PRAISE FOR *THE BULLET JOURNAL METHOD*

"Bullet journaling is one of the most elegant and effective productivity systems I've ever encountered. It will not only help you get more organized but will also help you become a better person. I highly recommend this book (and the method it details) for anyone looking to get more out of life."

—Cal Newport, author of *Deep Work*

"Whether you are an avid journaler or have always wanted to explore the benefits of journaling, *The Bullet Journal Method* simplifies the power of putting pen to paper and will undoubtedly transform your life, in more ways than you can imagine."

—Hal Elrod, author of *The Miracle Morning*

"Ryder has done an extraordinary job in sharing a comprehensive and hands-on methodology to implement the powerful practice of externalizing our thinking—no matter what it's about! It's a great treatise and manual for freeing and directing our consciousness, with lots of tips about how to play in that big and wonderful game."

—David Allen, author of *Getting Things Done*

THE
BULLET⚡JOURNAL
METHOD

TRACK THE PAST,

ORDER THE PRESENT,

DESIGN THE FUTURE

RYDER CARROLL

PORTFOLIO • PENGUIN

Portfolio/Penguin
An imprint of Penguin Random House LLC
375 Hudson Street
New York, New York 10014

Most Portfolio books are available at a discount when purchased in quantity for sales
promotions or corporate use. Special editions, which include personalized covers, excerpts,
and corporate imprints, can be created when purchased in large quantities. For more
information, please call (212) 572-2232 or e-mail specialmarkets@penguinrandomhouse.com.
Your local bookstore can also assist with discounted bulk purchases using
the Penguin Random House corporate Business-to-Business program. For assistance
in locating a participating retailer, e-mail B2B@penguinrandomhouse.com.

ISBN: 9780525533337 (hardcover)
ISBN: 9780525533344 (ebook)

Printed in the United States of America
5   7   9   10   8   6   4

Book design by Meighan Cavanaugh

TO MY PARENTS FOR JUST ABOUT EVERYTHING

TO THE BULLET JOURNAL COMMUNITY
FOR DARING

THANK YOU,

RYDER

INDEX

T.O.C. vs. Index: In the Bullet Journal we combine the table of contents and a traditional index to keep the content in your notebook organized and easily accessible. You can read more about this on page 99.

Let us postpone nothing. Let us balance life's account every day. . . . One who daily puts the finishing touches to his life is never in want of time.

—SENECA, *Moral Letters to Lucilius*

I

THE PREPARATION

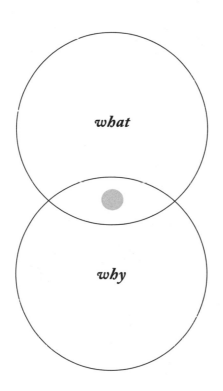

what

why

INTRODUCTION

The mystery box arrived unannounced. Stranger still, there was my mother's unmistakable block script adorning the address label. Maybe a surprise gift, for no particular occasion or reason? Unlikely.

Opening the box revealed a mess of old notebooks. Perplexed, I fished out a nuclear orange one covered in graffiti. Its pages brimmed with rough illustrations of robots, monsters, battle scenes, and wildly misspelled words. Different kinds of . . . a chill went down my spine. These were mine!

I took a deep breath and dove in. This was more than a trip down memory lane. It was like reentering the husk of an all-but-forgotten self. As I leafed through another notebook, a folded sheet fell from its pages. Curious, I unfolded it to find a grotesque rendering of a very angry man. He was yelling so hard that his eyes bulged and his tongue flapped out of his mouth. Two words were written on the page. One small word, shyly tucked into a corner, revealed the identity of the apoplectic man: an old teacher of mine. The other large jagged word, the one revealing the target of his rage, was my name.

My problems started early in elementary school with the terrible grades, the red-faced teachers, the resigned tutors. My performance was so alarming that I spent a good amount of my summers in special schools and psychologists' offices. Eventually I was diagnosed with attention deficit disorder (ADD). This was back in the 1980s, when mullets were better understood than my condition. The few resources that were available were either too complicated or proscriptive to prove helpful, or didn't fit my needs. If anything, they salted the wound. Nothing worked the way that my mind worked, so I was left largely to my own dull devices.

The main culprit was my inability to rein in my focus. It wasn't that I couldn't focus; I just had a hard time concentrating on the right thing at the right time, on being present. My attention would always dart off to the next bright thing. As I cycled through distractions, my responsibilities steadily piled up until they became overwhelming. I often found myself coming up short or trailing behind. Facing those feelings day in, day out led to deep self-doubt. Few things are more distracting than the cruel stories we tell ourselves.

I admired my successful peers, with their unwavering attention and their notebooks brimming with detailed notes. I became fascinated with order and discipline, qualities that to me seemed as beautiful as they did foreign. To unravel these mysteries, I started devising organizational tricks designed to embrace the way *my* mind worked.

Through trial and *a lot* of error, I gradually pieced together a system that worked, all in my good old-fashioned paper notebook. It was a cross between a planner, diary, notebook, to-do list, and sketchbook. It provided me with a practical yet forgiving tool to organize my impatient mind. Gradually, I became less distracted, less overwhelmed, and a lot more productive. I realized that it was up to me to solve my challenges. More importantly, I realized that I could!

By 2007, I was working as a web designer for a big fashion label headquartered in the neon heart of New York City, Times Square. I'd gotten the job through a friend who worked there and was struggling to plan her upcoming wedding. Her desk was littered with notebooks, Post-its, and scraps of paper a couple of inches deep. It looked like one of those manic conspiracy map rooms you see in crime shows.

I'd been looking for a way to repay her for getting me the position. So one day, as I saw her scrounging for yet another wayward note, I awkwardly offered to show her how I used my notebook. She turned to me with raised eyebrows, and to my surprise—and horror—she took me up on the offer. Gulp. What had I gotten myself into? Sharing my notebook was like offering someone an unadulterated look into my mind, which, well . . . yeah.

A few days later we went for coffee. My clumsy tutorial took a while. I felt deeply vulnerable exposing how I organized my thoughts—the symbols, the systems, the templates, the cycles, the lists. To me, these were the many crutches invented to support a faulty brain. I avoided making eye contact until I was finished. Mortified, I looked up. Her gaping mouth instantly validated all my insecurities. After an excruciating pause she said, "You have to share this with people."

After the awkwardness of that tutorial, it took a lot more prodding for me to share my system. But over the years, I found myself fielding shy questions from designers, developers, project managers, and accountants about my ever-present notebook. Some asked about organizing their day-to-day. So I showed them how to use my system for quickly logging their tasks, events, and notes. Others asked about setting goals. So I demonstrated how they could use my system for structuring action plans to tackle future aims. Others just wanted to be less scattered, so I showed them how to neatly funnel all their notes and projects into one notebook.

It had never occurred to me that these solutions I'd devised could be so widely applicable. If someone had a specific need, it was easy to modify one of my techniques to support it. I started to wonder whether sharing my solutions to common organizational challenges might help others avoid, or at least mitigate, the frustration I had endured earlier in my life.

All well and good, but if I was going to open my mouth again, there would be no more awkward freestyling. I formalized the system and streamlined it, stripping away everything but the most effective techniques I had developed over the years. Nothing exactly like it existed, so I had to invent a new language with its own vocabulary. This made the system significantly easier to explain—and, I hoped, to learn. Now it needed a name, something that spoke to its speed, its efficiency, its heritage, and its purpose. I called it the Bullet Journal.

Next, I launched a website featuring interactive tutorials and videos that walked users through the newly minted Bullet Journal system, aka BuJo. I smiled when the site passed 100 unique visitors. To me, that was mission accomplished! Then the unexpected happened. Bulletjournal.com was featured on Lifehack.org. Then on Lifehacker.com, then in *Fast Company*, and from there it went viral. The site went from 100 to 100,000 unique visitors in *days*.

Bullet Journal communities sprouted up across the web. To my astonishment, people were openly sharing their approaches to dealing with deeply personal challenges. Veterans shared their tactics for coping with PTSD by tracking their days in their Bullet Journals. People suffering from OCD shared ways to distance themselves from their overpowering thoughts. I was touched hearing from those like myself suffering from ADD as they shared how their grades improved and their anxiety diminished. In the often toxic world of online communities, these Bullet Journal groups created incredibly positive and supportive spaces, each focusing on different challenges, all using the same tool.

Sandy stumbled upon Bullet Journaling in May 2017, through a video on Facebook. Lack of sleep and caring for a toddler left her extremely disorganized and forgetful, which is not how anyone would normally describe her. Thoughts ran through her mind like squirrels: Had he slept long enough? Were his immunizations on track? When was that preschool application deadline again? As soon as she put one task to rest, another popped up in its place. She felt stressed and demoralized. Did other moms know something she didn't? So when she heard about an organizational system requiring just a notebook and a pen, she felt she had nothing to lose.

The first step was to create a log of everything she had to do that month. She wrote each family member's schedule in separate columns. They all worked irregular hours. It felt like she could finally press pause on the roller coaster for long enough to see who would be where for the next four weeks. It was horrifying to think about how easily one of them could forget to pick up their baby from preschool in a few years. It felt like it was just a matter of time before they would forget something important.

Sandy resolutely drew another column. She wrote down events and birthdays so they were easily visible. On her monthly financial log, she listed when bills were due and how much she'd paid. She also added daily boxes to track habits and goals—or just a reminder to stop and breathe!

Writing by hand was strangely soothing. Sandy didn't want to set her hopes too high, though, when so many other systems had promised to get the organized side of herself back without delivering long-term change.

Sandy moved on to the next part of the instructions. They were intended to help her keep sight of the bigger picture. What were her aspirations for the coming year? On her Yearly Goals page, she dared to write down a passion project that she'd been weakly attempting for years—with no progress to show for it. Was her OCD sabotaging her resolution to spend more time lettering and drawing? Or was she just too busy? All she knew was that she had potential she wasn't using.

Over the coming weeks, Sandy's habit of sitting down with her Bullet Journal became as effortless as brushing her teeth. Silly as it seemed, crossing off little boxes kept her motivated by reminding her that there was a finite number of tasks to do every day. She didn't forget about a single bill. Nor did she have to send any long, apologetic texts for forgetting someone's birthday. Another surprising thing was that the layout of the Bullet Journal reminded her that mundane tasks were part of the bigger picture. The Monthly Goals and Yearly Goals pages showed her every day that she had a long game, and that she was on her way. Her trick was to add a tiny passion project—say, 15 minutes of lettering by hand—to every Daily Log, and to do it first thing every day. She always had 15 free minutes if she took them before checking her phone. It was like time had expanded.

Soon Sandy noticed that journaling garnered more benefits than just keeping her organized and sane. All her life, she'd suffered from a condition called dermatillomania, also known as compulsive skin-picking disorder, that she'd been ashamed of her whole life. For Sandy, it was mostly concentrated on her fingers. She'd canceled meetings and interviews because she felt her fingers looked horrible. Sometimes she couldn't sleep because of the pain, and she'd constantly dropped things and was unable to do the simplest of tasks. For example, she'd always asked her husband or her mom to help her squeeze some lemon for her tea to avoid the biting pain of the acidic sting.

After Bullet Journaling for a few months, she found herself in the kitchen, tears welling up in her eyes. She looked down at her hands, finally squeezing a lemon, and realized that her fingers were no longer covered with wounds. With every line, letter, and notation she made, she'd kept her hands busy and let them slowly but surely heal. I've included the special page she designed in her journal to commemorate the day.

Not only did Bullet Journaling help her plan, track, and keep memories; it let her be creative, heal and no longer hide, and be a part of an encouraging, supportive community. She is not alone in this. I've also been inspired by the inventive, resilient, and spirited Bullet Journalists who have taken my methodology and customized it to fit their circumstances. This is in part why I decided to write this book.

Whether you're an experienced Bullet Journalist or a newcomer, *The Bullet Journal Method* is for anyone struggling to find their

15.12.17

SQUEEZED A LEMON

— NO —

stinging

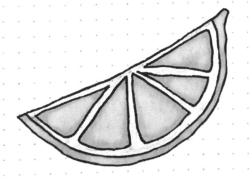

place in the digital age. It will help you get organized by providing simple tools and techniques that can inject clarity, direction, and focus into your days. As great as getting organized feels, however, it's just the surface of something significantly deeper and more valuable.

I had always thought my ADD made me different from others. One thing this community helped me realize is that my condition simply forced me to address something early on that has since become a common malady of the digital age: the lack of self-awareness.

In the most connected time in history, we're quickly losing touch with ourselves. Overwhelmed by a never-ending flood of information, we're left feeling overstimulated yet restless, overworked yet discontented, tuned in yet burned out. As technology leaked into every nook in my life, with its countless distractions, my methodology provided an analog refuge that proved invaluable in helping me define and focus on what truly mattered. Now countless others have found it key in helping them reclaim agency over their lives.

In 2015, Anthony Gorrity, a shy designer, quit an unsatisfying agency job and started freelancing. He'd been dreaming of going out on his own for years. What he didn't anticipate was the added pressure to perform and the need to structure his own time. He tried a few apps to keep himself organized, but none were as flexible as he needed. He took to keeping notebooks of to-do lists, but they were a mess. Clients would call him without warning, and he'd rifle through six different notebooks trying to find the notes he needed. He knew he'd written this down . . . somewhere. . . . All of these frantic moments undercut his confidence. As someone who wasn't a natural self-promoter, he had a hard enough time pitching himself to get work—and now it seemed as if once the work came in, a whole new set of stressful challenges awaited. He wondered if he'd made a mistake by going freelance. Then he had a distant memory of seeing a video of some guy demoing some super-complex journal system that he swore by. He started Googling all kinds of weird keywords until he eventually found BulletJournal.com. The system wasn't nearly as complex as he'd remembered. He grabbed a fresh notebook and started consolidating everything he needed to do.

A few things changed. He became a lot more introspective. He realized that he *loved* making to-do lists, and he loved knocking out tasks even more. Best of all, self-confidence had room to take root in the clean, clear space of his notebook: Having things written down gave him the guts he needed when on the phone with a client. Being prepared, and knowing his material, made him feel less like a salesman and more like a craftsman. The Bullet Journal provided a framework that allowed Anthony to explore his potential.

This is a critical aspect of the methodology; it helps us cultivate a better sense of ourselves both in and out of the professional theater. The simple act of pausing to write down the important minutia of one's life goes far beyond simple organization. It has helped people reconnect with themselves and the things they care about.

I spend much of my time nowadays connecting with fellow Bullet Journalists like Sandy and Anthony and fielding questions from the community. Many seek to expand the functionality of their Bullet Journals. Others delve deeper, tackling universal challenges that have become amplified in today's frenetic world. In this book, I seek to address those questions and demonstrate how a simple notebook can prove invaluable in uncovering the answers.

The Bullet Journal method consists of two parts: the system and the practice. First we'll learn about the system, to teach you how to transform your notebook into a powerful organizational tool. Then we'll examine the practice. It's a fusion of philosophies from a variety of traditions that define how to live an intentional life—a life both productive and purposeful. The result of my endeavor to translate this timeless knowledge into focused action resulted in the Bullet Journal method, the analog system for the digital age. It will help you track the past and order the present so that you can design your future. I originally developed it as a way to overcome my organizational challenges. Over the years, though, it's matured into a personal operating system that has profoundly changed my life for the better. My hope is that it can do the same for you.

THE PROMISE

*Life had gotten too busy. It seemed as if my
existence had become just one long to-do list.
I had forgotten about my dreams, my goals,
my what-ifs, my "what if I could's."*

—AMY HAINES

The Bullet Journal method's mission is to help us become mindful about how we spend our two most valuable resources in life: our time and our energy. If you're going to invest both reading this book, it's only fair to start by highlighting what's in it for you. To sum it up:

*The Bullet Journal method will help you
accomplish more by working on less. It helps
you identify and focus on what is meaningful
by stripping away what is meaningless.*

How does it do this? By weaving together productivity, mindfulness, and intentionality into a framework that is flexible, forgiving, and, most importantly, practical. Let's take a closer look at each.

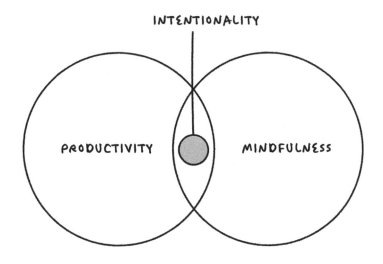

Productivity

Do you ever feel overwhelmed by all your responsibilities? Sometimes life feels like a hellish game of whack-a-mole, condemned to stomping out never-ending chores, meetings, emails, and texts. Your multitasking madness has you squeezing in workouts by pacing across your apartment while FaceTiming your sister—who is asking if you could breathe less heavily. Nothing is getting the attention it deserves, and it doesn't feel good. You hate disappointing other people as much as you hate disappointing yourself. To get more done, you've even hacked your sleep, whittling it down to the bare minimum—except now you're a zombie because . . . you've hacked your sleep down to the bare minimum.

Let's step back. Every year between 1950 and 2000, Americans increased their productivity about 1 to 4 percent.[1] Since 2005, however, this growth has slowed in advanced economies, with a productivity *decrease* recorded in the United States in 2016.[2] Maybe our rapidly evolving technology that promises us near-limitless options to keep us busy is not, in fact, making us more productive?

One possible explanation for our productivity slowdown is that we're paralyzed by information overload. As Daniel Levitin writes in *The Organized Mind*, information overload is worse for our focus than exhaustion or smoking marijuana.[3]

It stands to reason, then, that to be more productive we need a way to stem the tide of digital distractions. Enter the Bullet Journal, an analog solution that provides the offline space needed to process, to think, and to focus. When you open your notebook, you automatically unplug. It momentarily pauses the influx of information so your mind can catch up. Things become less of a blur, and you can finally examine your life with greater clarity.

The Bullet Journal will help you declutter your packed mind so you can finally examine your thoughts from an objective distance.

We often cobble together ways to organize ourselves on the fly. A little of this app; a little of that calendar. Over time, this results in an unwieldy productivity Frankenstein of Post-its, various apps, and email. It kinda works, but it also feels like it's coming apart at the seams. You waste time deliberating where information should go and trying to locate it later: Did you write something down in your notes app or on a Post-it? And where did that Post-it go, anyway?

Many a great idea, "keeper" thought, or important "note to self" has fallen victim to a misplaced scrap of paper or an outdated app. It's a compounding inefficiency that drains your bandwidth, but it's completely avoidable. The Bullet Journal is designed to be your "source of truth." No, this is not some dubious invitation to worship this methodology. It means that you no longer have to wonder where your thoughts live.

Once you've learned how to keep your thoughts in one place, we'll examine how to prioritize them effectively. Everyone calling, emailing, or texting you wants your answer right away. Rather than being proactive about setting priorities, a lot of us simply let the flood of external demands set them for us. Distracted and over-extended, our opportunities go under. There goes your chance to increase your GPA, to get that promotion, to run that marathon, to read a book every two weeks.

BuJo puts you at the helm. You'll learn how to stop reacting and start responding.

You'll learn how to tackle difficult challenges and turn your vague curiosities into meaningful goals, how to break your goals into smaller, more manageable Sprints, and then finally how to effectively take action. What's the next step to improving your GPA this semester? Acing all your classes? No. Get more granular. In which class are you falling behind? What's the next assignment in that class? Writing a paper. Okay, what book do you need to read before writing that paper? Getting that book from the library—*that's* the most important thing you have to do *now*. What about doing the extra-credit assignment for the class you're already acing? Waste of time.

In this book, we will introduce scientifically proven techniques that turn any notebook into a powerful tool for surfacing opportunities and weeding out distractions so that you can focus your time and energy on what actually matters.

Mindfulness

Uh-oh, the "M" word. Don't worry, no sitars required. When we talk about mindfulness, we're typically talking about a heightened awareness of the present. Productivity is all fine and good, but BuJo isn't designed to help you spin faster on the hamster wheel.

We live in an age where technology promises us near-limitless options to occupy ourselves, yet we're left feeling more distracted and disconnected than ever before. Like when flying, we watch the world speed by at 600 miles an hour with no idea where we truly are. If we're lucky, we may glimpse some ocean glinting below or lightning ripping through dark distant clouds. For the most part, though, we're semiconscious passengers, killing time before the unnerving descent.

If the journey is the destination, then we must learn how to become better travelers. To become better travelers, we must first learn to orient ourselves. Where are you now? Do you want to be here? If not, why do you want to move on?

*To successfully navigate the world
around us, we must look inward.*

Mindfulness is the process of waking up to see what's right in front of us. It helps you become more aware of where you are, who you are, and what you want. This is where BuJo comes into play. The act of writing by hand draws our mind into the present moment on a neurological level unlike any other capturing mechanism.[4] It is in the present moment that we begin to know ourselves. Joan Didion, a famous proponent of writing things down, began doing so at age five. She believed that notebooks were one of the best antidotes for a distracted world: "We forget all too soon the things we thought we could never forget. We forget the loves and the betrayals alike, forget what we whispered and what we screamed, forget who we were. . . . It is a good idea, then, to keep in touch, and I suppose that keeping in touch is what notebooks are all about. And we are all on our own when it comes to keeping those lines open to ourselves: your notebook will never help me, nor mine you."[5]

For you digital natives out there, fear not. Banish the image of some hunched, squint-eyed Dickensian figure endlessly scrawling away in a garret by failing candlelight. No, here you'll learn how to capture thoughts quickly and effectively. You'll learn how to journal at the speed of life.

This is where BuJo comes into play. We'll explore various techniques that help us form the habit of asking these kinds of questions, so we stop getting lost in the daily grind. In other words, the Bullet Journal method keeps us mindful of *why* we're doing *what* we're doing.

Intentionality

Think back to a book, a speech, or a quotation that deeply touched you or changed the way you thought about life. It was wisdom that inspired you, that held so much promise. All you had to do was act on this newfound knowledge and things would get easier, better, clearer, more empowering.

Now, how much of this knowledge is still in play—not just intellectually, but practically? Did you become a better person, friend, or mate? Did you keep the weight off? Are you happier? Chances are what you learned has withered, if it survived at all. It's not that it wasn't helpful. It just didn't stick. Why is that?

The rush of our busy lives can quietly carve out a gulf separating our actions from our beliefs. We tend to follow the path of least resistance, even when it leads away from the things we care about. It can require a lot of ongoing effort to effect the change we seek. As any athlete will tell you, you need to tear muscle to build it, over and over again. Like building muscle, we need to train our intentions to make them resilient and strong.

Whereas it's easy to "forget" to meditate or summon excuses to skip yoga, there are serious and immediate repercussions when we ignore our day-to-day obligations. To successfully introduce a new sustainable routine, it needs to fit into your packed schedule. What if you had a way that championed your intentions *and* kept you more organized throughout your day?

The Bullet Journal method acts as a bridge between your beliefs and your actions by integrating into the nitty-gritty of your life.

In addition to organizing her obligations, Amy Haines used her Bullet Journal to keep track of ideas for her business, people she wanted to learn from, apps to check out, even new teas to try. She customized her Collections—which you'll read about later—to cut through the sinking feeling of endless to-do lists and to stay in touch with what she really wanted to do. She was able to reclaim the things that mattered and had gotten away.

Through Bullet Journaling, you'll automatically form a regular habit of introspection where you'll begin to define *what's* important, *why* it's important, and then figure out *how* to best pursue those things. You're gently reminded of these insights every day, which makes it easier to put them into action wherever you happen to be, be it a boardroom, classroom, or even an emergency room.

Bullet Journalists have been hired for dream jobs, started businesses, ended toxic relationships, relocated, or, in some cases, simply become more content with who they are by making BuJo part of their routine. This methodology is powered by wisdom from traditions around the world. Like a reverse prism, Bullet Journal absorbs these traditions and focuses them into one bright beam that will help you clearly see where you are and illuminate the way forward. It will empower you to go from passenger to pilot through the art of intentional living.

THE GUIDE

Bullet Journaling is not a fair-weather friend. It has dutifully suffered and celebrated alongside me through all the different seasons of my life. It has served the many masters of my former selves: the student, the intern, the heartbroken, the designer, and more. It always welcomes me without judgment or expectation. When setting out to write this book, I wanted to create something that could serve you the same way. This book is designed as your Bullet Journal base camp. It's here to prepare you for your first ascent and to welcome you back when you need to rest, restock, and recalibrate.

GEAR

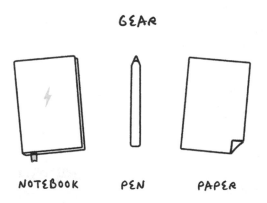

NOTEBOOK   PEN   PAPER

For Those Just Getting Started

If this is your first experience with the Bullet Journal, welcome! Thank you kindly for spending your time here. To get the most from this book, I encourage you to follow the linear path, beginning to end. This path is designed to be participatory. We'll leverage the power of transcription (page 47) to help you imprint the system faster into your mind. All you'll need is a blank sheet of paper, an empty notebook, and something to write with.

The Bullet Journal method is comprised of two main components: the system and the practice. Part II of this book will focus on the system. You'll learn the names of the ingredients and how they're used. Like in a kitchen, Parts I and II will help you become a skilled line cook. Parts III and IV are where we delve into the practice. There you'll learn how to become a chef. We'll explore the sources and science behind these ingredients so that you can customize the Bullet Journal to suit your needs.

For Seasoned Bullet Journalists— and Anyone in Between

The chapters are designed as independent Collections (page 84), mimicking the structure of the Bullet Journal system. As long as you're comfortable with the BuJo vocabulary, you should be able to open the book to any chapter that grabs your attention. If you're not, then check out Part II!

Part II delves into the system that you know and love in great detail. We take a closer look at each core Collection and technique, revealing both the reasoning and history behind their design. Then, in Part IV, we apply all of these concepts to a mock project. Here you'll learn how to extend and further customize the system.

The system, however, is only one part of what makes up the Bullet Journal method.

*The first parts of this book are about **how** to Bullet Journal. The latter parts are about **why** to Bullet Journal.*

If you've been Bullet Journaling for a while, you may have felt there's more to it than just keeping your lists organized. You may feel that it's made you more grounded, confident, focused, calmer, even inspired. That's because the Bullet Journal is powered by various sciences and philosophies to help us live with more intention. In this book, I'll pull back the curtain to reveal why the Bullet Journal has the effect that it does. This deeper context will not only validate what you're already doing, but can take your BuJo practice to a whole new level.

Whatever level you're at, from BuJo newbie to pro, this book is a look into the heart of Bullet Journaling, where mindfulness meets productivity to help you design a life you want to live.

THE WHY

*Intentional living is the art of making our own
choices before others' choices make us.*

—RICHIE NORTON

My first start-up, Paintapic, was born in a closet filled with thousands of thimble-size pots of paint. The service allowed you to turn your photos into a custom paint-by-number kit, complete with a canvas, paints, and brushes. At the time, I also had a demanding full-time day job, so Paintapic was built entirely on nights and weekends.

Leadership had changed at my nine-to-five, and the new direction had pulled the plug on the creative projects that allowed me to enjoy my job. Over time, this new vision became so limiting that I no longer felt I was adding real value to the company. My potential impact on Paintapic, however, was limited only by the amount of time I was willing to invest. So I Old Yellered my social life for Paintapic's sake and got to work.

My cofounder had convinced his employer to rent us an unused storage closet . . . as our office. That dark room with its one small frosted window devoured our nights and weekends for nearly two years. Thousands of decisions were made in that cramped Cyclopean skull of a room. We poured ourselves into every single detail—down to the number of bristles on our brushes.

Finally, the moment we had been waiting for arrived: launch day. Orders went out. Money came in. We were in the black. We were doing pretty well right out of the gate without any outside investment. That's rare for a start-up. We were by all accounts a (humble) success.

As soon as our site launched, I placed an order through our site. I remember how excited I was to receive my kit in the mail. Here it was, real and working! But by the time I had walked up the single flight of stairs to my flat, I was already preoccupied with something else. To this day, that kit remains unopened somewhere, a goofy portrait of a pug (our unofficial mascot) forever waiting to be painted.

My indifference quickly stained every aspect of running the company. Deep confusion and frustration set in. On paper, I had accomplished everything I was told would make me happy. I sacrificed a lot getting to this point, but now that I was here, it just didn't seem to matter. I wasn't alone. My partner seemed to share these feelings. The process of creating the company, the pleasure we got out of building, had blinded us to a simple truth: We were just not paint-by-number guys. Though the product added value to the lives of our customers, it added little to ours. We weren't passionate about the product—we'd just fallen in love with the entrepreneurial challenge.

How often do we find ourselves in this position? You've worked incredibly hard on something, only to discover that it leaves you feeling empty. You compensate by working even harder. You reason that maybe if you put in more hours, you'll finally be able to appreciate the fruits of your labor. Why does this happen?

What is your true motivation for lifting that weight, being on that diet, working so late? Are you trying to lose ten pounds for health reasons, or are you in a toxic relationship that's stripping you of your confidence? Maybe you don't realize that you're killing yourself at work just to put off having a hard conversation with your spouse. If that's the case, no matter how much time you clock at the office, it won't offer lasting relief, because you're climbing the wrong mountain. We need to understand what's actually driving our motivation *before* we ascend.

Our motivations are heavily informed by the media. Our social feeds are populated by endless images of wealth, travel, power, relaxation, beauty, pleasure, and Hollywood love. This virtual runoff perpetually seeps into our consciousness, polluting our sense of reality and self-worth every time we go online. We compare our lives to these largely artificial constructs and structure our plans accordingly, hoping to eventually afford a golden ticket to these misleading fantasies. Conveniently tucked out of sight are the months of planning, the "talent" lined up in audition studios toting their head shots, the production crews, the double-parked trucks filled with camera gear, the long spells of unemployment, the weeks of rain that stopped shooting, the food poisoning on location, the empty sets after they leave. Distracted by the never-ending stream of aspirational media, we forfeit our opportunity to define what is meaningful on our own terms.

Bronnie Ware, an Australian nurse and author who spent several years working in palliative care with patients in the last weeks of their lives, recorded her patients' top five regrets. The number one regret was that people wished they had stayed true to themselves.

When people realize that their life is almost over and look back clearly on it, it is easy to see how many dreams have gone unfulfilled. Most people had not honoured even a half of their dreams and had to die knowing that it was due to choices they had made, or not made.[6]

Choices come in all flavors: the good, the bad, the big, the small, the happy, and the hard choices to name but a few. We can make these choices carelessly, or we can make them with intention. But what does that mean? What does it mean to live an intentional life? The philosopher David Bentley Hart defines intentionality as "the fundamental power of the mind to direct itself toward something . . . a specific object, purpose, or end."[7] The term hails from medieval scholastic philosophy, so I'd like to adapt and update it a bit for our purposes: Intentionality is the power of the mind to direct itself toward that which it finds meaningful and take action toward that end.

If intentionality means acting according to your beliefs, then the opposite would be operating on autopilot. In other words, do you know why you're doing what you're doing?

We can't be true to ourselves if we don't know what *we* want, and more importantly *why*, so that's where we must begin. It's a process that requires the steady cultivation of our self-awareness. This may seem very woo-woo, but it can be as simple as paying attention to what resonates with us, what sparks our interest—and, just as importantly, what does not. As we begin to identify the things we're drawn to, we can start properly defining our dreams, based on what we actually believe in.

When we believe in what we're doing, we stop mindlessly clocking in. We become more innovative, creative, and present. We're not only working harder, but smarter because both our hearts and minds are genuinely engaged by the endeavor.

Cultivating this self-awareness is a lifelong process, but it starts by simply checking in with yourself. That's where the Bullet Journal method comes in. You can view your Bullet Journal as a living autobiography. It allows you to clearly see what the rush of life tends to obscure. You can track the decisions you've made, and the actions you've taken that led you to where you are. It encourages you to learn from your experiences. What worked, what did not, how did it make you feel, what's the next move? Day by day, you're deepening your self-awareness by becoming a steady witness to your story. With each page, you improve your ability to discern the meaningful from the meaningless. If you don't like how life is unfolding, you'll have developed the skill and determination required to change the narrative, as Rachael M. and her husband did:

I work full time as a graphic designer, run my own freelance business, and serve several days a week as a youth leader, all while helping my husband with his ministry. My husband and I met two years ago. We love being married, but almost from day one, there were so many needs and things to remember and events to schedule—we were both going crazy.

My husband and I were struggling to communicate and keep up-to-date with each other's schedule. I went to work, bought groceries on the way home, made food, cleaned house, and tried to remember everything else I had to get done. By then it was time for bed, and the next day we started all over again. In addition to all this, we learned that I had a thyroid condition, as well as gluten and lactose sensitivities. Now food prep was even harder. I was completely overwhelmed.

We also struggled to spend quality time together. That's obviously something that everyone knows is crucial to a happy, healthy marriage. However, since my husband is a pastor, a big part of his workweek happens on evenings and weekends and he takes time off during the typical workweek. I work a traditional nine-to-five Monday through Friday. It was extremely difficult to figure out how to carve out time together. I'm the extrovert of the relationship and I ended up feeling lonely a lot of the time because of how much his work needed him during my weekends.

We knew we had to do something, so we started scheduling everything in our Bullet Journals. We used the Weekly and Monthly Logs to get ahead of our schedule and figure out what was coming. This gave us a visual cue for how busy we were going to be and helped us know ahead of time when we probably needed to block off some time for just the two of us. It also helped me figure out that the key to feeling like I had enough time with him was having Saturdays together so we actually adjusted our schedules to ensure that both of us are protecting as many Saturdays as possible to spend time together.

Bullet Journaling helped us refocus on our personal goals as well. My husband and I were both single and established in careers we loved for some time before we got together. Both of us loving what we did meant we were used to giving our jobs a huge chunk of our attention, and that was important to us. We had to learn how to prioritize our marriage instead of just our work. We could have used digital calendars to sync up, but the discipline of analog and the experience of sitting down with our Bullet Journals to physically mark in events helped us have the conversations we needed to have and to look further ahead so we weren't always blindsided by the next thing. It also helped us express concerns if we were starting to schedule too many things outside the home. It made us feel like a unit, planning our life together, instead of trying to slam two busy calendars together. Now, we love our marriage and our jobs and want to help one another succeed professionally.

Now, almost eight months later, we are accomplishing more than ever in every area of our lives, all before 8:00 p.m. each night! Thanks to Bullet Journaling, I have a handle on my life. I know what's coming. I have built in moments to reflect and make sure I'm actually focusing on the right things. And I have new confidence in my marriage and ministry because I know my husband and I are on the same page and are working toward defined goals that we share—we've written them right in the front of our journals.

—Rachael M.

This is what it means to live an intentional life. It's not about living a perfect life, an easy life, or getting things right all the time. It's not even about being happy, though joy often greets you along this path. Leading an intentional life is about keeping your actions aligned with your beliefs. It's about penning a story that *you* believe in and that *you* can be proud of.

DECLUTTERING YOUR MIND

*Have nothing in your homes that you do not know
to be useful or believe to be beautiful.*

—WILLIAM MORRIS

S tudies have suggested that we have 50,000 to 70,000 thoughts per day.[8] For context, if each thought were a word, that means our minds are generating enough content to produce a book Every. Single. Day. Unlike a book, our thoughts are not neatly composed. On a good day they're vaguely coherent. This leaves our minds perpetually struggling to sort this gray matter gallimaufry. Where do you even begin? What comes first? Inevitably we find ourselves tackling too many things at the same time, spreading our focus so thin that nothing gets the attention it deserves. This is commonly referred to as "being busy." Being busy, however, is not the same thing as being productive.

*For most of us, "being busy" is code for being
functionally overwhelmed.*

What do I mean by that? We don't have time because we're working on a lot of things, yet things aren't working out a lot of the time. This phenomenon isn't just a twenty-first-century problem, but it has been exponentially exacerbated by the countless number of choices technology has put at our fingertips. Should we type, text, call, email, swipe, pin, tweet, Skype, FaceTime, Zoom, Message, or yell at our digital assistant to get it done, whatever it is? And in what order should all of that happen? (Oh, and before we can get started, we'll have to upgrade, update, reboot, log in, authenticate, reset our password, clear cookies, empty our cache, and sacrifice our firstborn before we can get where we're going . . . where was that again?)

This freedom of choice is a double-edged privilege. Every decision requires you to focus, and focus is an investment of your time and energy. Both are limited—and therefore exceptionally valuable—resources.

Warren Buffett, one of the most successful investors of all time, gave the following advice to his trusty pilot Mike Flint. They had been discussing Flint's long-term plans. Buffett asked Flint to draft a list of his top 25 career goals. When he was done, Buffett asked Flint to circle his top five. When asked about the ones he circled, Flint replied, "Well, the top five are my primary focus, but the other twenty come in a close second. They are still important, so I'll work on those intermittently as I see fit. They are not as urgent, but I still plan to give them a dedicated effort."

To which Buffett replied, "No. You've got it wrong, Mike. Everything you didn't circle just became your Avoid-At-All-Cost list. No matter what, these things get no attention from you until you've succeeded with your top five."[9]

In an interview published in *Vanity Fair*, President Barack Obama said, "You'll see I wear only gray or blue suits. I'm trying to pare down decisions. I don't want to make decisions about what I'm eating or wearing. Because I have too many other decisions to make."[10] The same is true of Facebook founder Mark Zuckerberg with his gray hoodies, or Apple founder Steve Jobs and his famous black-turtleneck-and-jeans uniform. Acutely aware of how taxing deliberating over options can be, they sought every opportunity to limit choice in their lives.

As psychologist Roy F. Baumeister wrote in his book *Willpower*: "No matter how rational and high-minded you try to be, you can't make decision after decision without paying a biological price. It's different from ordinary physical fatigue—you're not consciously aware of being tired—but you're low on mental energy."[11] This state is known as decision fatigue. In other words, the more decisions you have to make, the harder it becomes to make them well. This is why you're more likely to eat an unhealthy dinner at the end of the day than an unhealthy breakfast at the beginning of the day, when you have a full tank of willpower.

Left unchecked, decision fatigue can lead to decision avoidance. This is especially true for big life choices, which we tend to put off till the last minute. Daunting choices don't simply vanish; they wait in the wings, steadily becoming more menacing. Where do I want to go to college? Do I want to marry this person? Should I take that new job? By the time you're finally forced to make a decision, at the tail end of all the other decisions you've been making to avoid having to make this big one, chances are you don't have a lot of focus left to spare. No wonder we often feel stressed, anxious, and overwhelmed.

We try to treat these symptoms with even more distractions. Drinking, eating, traveling, binge-watching, etc. Even though your Netflix queue is four years long, somehow nothing looks good! You can't decide, and now you're even more stressed. In order to make a lasting difference, we need to address not the symptoms but the cause.

*We need to reduce the number of decisions
we burden ourselves with so we
can focus on what matters.*

The Mental Inventory

The first step to recovering from decision fatigue, to get out from under the pile of choices weighing on you, is to get some distance from them. You need some perspective to both clearly identify and corral your choices. We do this by writing them down. Why write them down? Each decision, until it's been made and acted on, is simply a thought. Holding on to thoughts is like trying to catch fish with your bare hands: They easily slip from your grasp and disappear back into the muddy depths of your mind. Writing things down allows us to capture our thoughts and examine them in the light of day. By externalizing our thoughts, we begin to declutter our minds. Entry by entry, we're creating a mental inventory of all the choices consuming our attention. It's the first step to taking back control over our lives. Here is where you can begin to filter out the signal from the noise. Here is where your Bullet Journal journey will begin.

Just like when organizing a closet, we need to take everything out before we can decide what stays and what goes. Creating a mental inventory is a simple technique that will help you quickly take stock of what you've been jamming into your mental closet. Chances are there are a lot of useless responsibilities hogging valuable mental and emotional real estate up there.

To begin, sit down with that sheet of paper I mentioned you'd be needing. Orient it horizontally and divide it into three columns (you can either fold it twice or draw the lines like in the Mental Inventory on page 39).

1. In the first column, list all the things you are presently working on.
2. In the second, list all the things you *should* be working on.
3. In the last column, list the things you *want* to be working on.

Keep your entries short and in list form. If one task sparks a stream of others, go with it. Give yourself some time with this exercise, and dig deep. Be honest. Get it out of your head (and your heart) and lay it out on the page. Take a deep breath and begin.

MENTAL INVENTORY

Working on	Should be working on	Want to be working on
Taxes	Workout plan	Plan trip to Hawaii
Presentation for Acme Co.	Learn how to invest	Learn to cook
Cleaning up photo library	Weekly meal plans	Learn another language
Emmy dinner party planning	Set 5-year goal	Read more
	Call Parents	Write more
	Get a checkup	Lose 10 pounds
	Retirement plan	More time with friends

The Test

This Mental Inventory you just created provides a clear picture of how you're currently investing your time and energy. It's a map of your choices. The next step is to figure out which ones are worth making.

We're so busy with all the things we're doing (or should be doing) that we forget to ask ourselves *why* we're doing these things. We end up burdening ourselves with all sorts of unnecessary responsibilities. The Mental Inventory grants us the opportunity to take a step back and ask why.

Go ahead, ask why for each item on your list. You don't need to dive down an existential rabbit hole. Simply ask yourself two questions:

1. Does this matter? (To you *or* to someone you love)
2. Is this vital? (Think rent, taxes, student loans, your job, etc.)

TIP: If you struggle to answer these questions about a given item, ask yourself what would happen if said item just didn't get done. *Ever.* Would there be any real repercussions?

Any item that doesn't pass this test is a distraction. It adds little to no value to your life. Cross it off. Be ruthless. Keep in mind that each task is an experience waiting to be born, offering a glimpse into your potential future. That's why everything on your list has to fight for its life to stay there. More accurately, each item needs to fight for the opportunity to become part of your life.

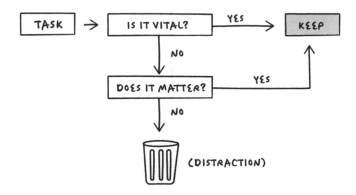

When you're done, you'll probably be left with two types of tasks: things you *need* to do (your responsibilites) and things you *want* to do (that is, your goals). Throughout the course of this book, I will show you ways you can push forward on both fronts. For now, though, you have all the ingredients needed to populate your Bullet Journal. All, that is, except for your notebook.

Now you may be asking, *Why didn't we just do this in our note-book?* It's a fair question. As you read this book, ponder the ideas, and try out the techniques, you might find yourself paring back your Mental Inventory even more. When you christen your Bullet Journal, you should do so with only things that you believe are important or will add value to your life. Being intentional about what you let into your life is a practice that shouldn't be limited to the pages of your notebook.

NOTEBOOKS

Journal writing is a voyage to the interior.
—CHRISTINA BALDWIN

People who are new to BuJo often ask about the notebook. Can't we just use an app for keeping lists? The short answer is sure. In fact, there are a lot of good productivity apps out there. I worked on some myself! As a digital product designer, I can fully appreciate how powerful and effective digital tools can be. In fact, the Bullet Journal was designed using some methodologies leveraged in software development. That said, there's a lot more to Bullet Journaling than keeping lists. It's a comprehensive methodology designed to help us capture, order, and examine our experience. As you move through this book, you'll see exactly how and why your notebook will serve you well in this regard. Here, we'll look at the foundational reasons behind the notebook.

Technology removes barriers and distances between people and information. We can learn about almost anything, or communicate with anyone, at any time, from anywhere, just by tapping our phone. It's a convenience that we avail ourselves of, on average, every 12 minutes![12] All of this convenience, however, comes at a price—and I don't mean the cost of your data plan, your cable bundle, or the pieces of your soul you sacrifice as you try to reason with your provider's customer service.

In a world where Wi-Fi boosters are attached to church steeples, no place remains sacred.[13] From the boardroom to the bathroom, technology has flooded our lives with more content than we can possibly absorb, washing away our attention spans in the process. Studies suggest that your concentration suffers simply by having your smartphone in the room with you, even if it's silent or powered off![14]

In 2016, the average American spent nearly eleven hours in front of digital screens each day.[15] Factoring in six to eight hours of sleep (which is also compromised by our phones[16]), we're left with around six hours of non-screen time per day. Now consider the time spent commuting, cooking, and running errands, and you can see where this is headed: We're steadily decreasing the amount of time we have to stop and think.

Sitting down with your notebook grants you that precious luxury. It provides a personal space, free from distraction, where you can get to know yourself better. This is one of the main reasons we use a notebook to Bullet Journal: It forces us to go offline.

Our notebook serves as a mental sanctuary where we are free to think, reflect, process, and focus.

The blank pages of your notebook offer a safe playground for your mind, where you're completely free to express yourself without judgment or expectation. As soon as you put pen to paper, you establish a direct link to your mind and often your heart. This experience has yet to be properly replicated in the digital space. It's why, to this day, so many ideas are born on scraps of paper.

Another reason we use notebooks? Flexibility. Software tends to be either so powerful that its wealth of features is buried to all but the most intrepid explorers (think Excel) or so specific that it sacrifices features for increased usability, essentially doing few things very well (think mobile apps). In both cases, they force you to operate within a framework of *their* choosing. This is the main challenge with many productivity systems: They struggle to address the limitless variability and evolutionary nature of our individual needs. Notebooks, in contrast, are beholden to their authors. Their function is limited only by the imagination of their owner.

The power of the Bullet Journal is that it becomes whatever you need it to be, no matter what season of life you're in.

In school, it can serve for your class notes. At work, it can be a tool to organize your projects. At home, it can help you set and track your goals. Robyn C., for example, was able to meditate for 432 *consecutive* days by designing a meditation tracker in her Bullet Journal. She did the same when trying to figure out what triggered her sleeping disorder. I didn't invent her tools; she did.

Because of the way the Bullet Journal is structured, it can be multiple things at the same time. Rather than a tool, think of it as a tool kit. It allows you to funnel a lot of your productivity needs into one place. You'll enjoy a more comprehensive perspective on your life, one that can allow you to spot unconventional connections. As Bullet Journalist Bert Webb put it: "As I do daily, weekly, and monthly reviews, leafing forward and backward in my Bullet Journal, my brain inevitably makes more links between ideas that I was not able to do when using my various separate digital tools."

The other great thing is that you start fresh each day. With digital trackers, you step onto their track—somewhere in the middle of the endless race that started when you set up the tracker and ends . . . ? Your notebook greets you each morning with the pure, blank slate of an empty page. It serves as a small reminder that the day is as yet unwritten. It will become what you make of it. As Bullet Journalist Kevin D. notes: "I used to feel bad about items undone at the end of the day, but with the Bullet Journal I feel empowered to move yesterday's open bullets forward to a new page, because I see each day as a fresh start."

Finally, your notebook evolves as you do. You might say that you co-iterate. It will conform to your ever-changing needs. The lovely side effect is that as the years pass, you're creating a record of your choices, and the ensuing experiences. As Bullet Journalist Kim Alvarez once put it, "Each Bullet Journal contributes another volume to a library of your life." In the pursuit of meaning, this library becomes a powerful resource to have at your disposal.

By recording our lives, we're simultaneously creating a rich archive of our choices and our actions for future reference. We can study our mistakes and learn from them. It's equally instructive to note our successes, our breakthroughs. When something works professionally or personally, it helps to know what our circumstances were at the time and what choices we made. Studying our failures and our victories can provide tremendous insight, guidance, and motivation as we plot our way forward.

So are the Bullet Journal method and apps mutually exclusive? Of course not. There are many apps that make my life easier in ways that a notebook never could. All tools, whether digital or analog, are only as valuable as their ability to help you accomplish the task at hand. The goal of this book is to introduce you to a new tool kit for your workshop—one that has proven effective at helping countless others tackle the often ungainly project called life.

HANDWRITING

The palest ink is better than the best memory.
—CHINESE PROVERB

We breathe life into our thoughts by committing them to paper. Be they words, images, or notes, few tools facilitate the transition between the inner and outer worlds as seamlessly as the tip of a pen. In a world moving toward untextured interfaces, it may seem like an awkward step backward to implement a methodology that requires you to write things out the old-fashioned way. But a growing body of research points to the continued practicality of the handwritten word in our digital age.

A University of Washington study demonstrated that elementary school students who wrote essays by hand were far more likely to write in fully formed sentences and learn how to read faster. Much of this is due to how handwriting accelerates and deepens our ability to form—and therefore recognize—characters.[17]

The complex tactile movement of writing by hand stimulates our mind more effectively than typing. It activates multiple regions of the brain simultaneously, thereby imprinting what we learn on a deeper level. As a result, we retain information longer than we would by tapping it into an app.[18] In one study, college students who were asked to take lecture notes by hand tested better on average than those who had typed out their notes. They were also able to better retain this information long after the exam.[19]

When we put pen to paper, we're not just turning on the lights; we're also turning up the heat. Writing by hand helps us think and feel simultaneously.

These studies and many like them indicate that the benefits of writing by hand stem from the very complaint consistently leveraged against it: inefficiency. That's right: The fact that it takes longer to write things out by hand gives handwriting its cognitive edge.

It's pretty much impossible to hand-transcribe lectures or meetings verbatim. When we write by hand, we're forced to be more economical and strategic with our use of language, crafting notes in our own words. To do that, we have to listen more closely, think about the information, and essentially distill others' words and thoughts through our own neurological filtration system and onto the page. Typing notes, in contrast, can quickly become rote: a frictionless highway where information freely passes in one ear and right out the other.

Why is it so important to craft notes in your own words? The science suggests that writing by hand enhances the way we engage with information, strengthening our associative thinking. It allows us to form new connections that can yield unconventional solutions and insights. We're simultaneously expanding our awareness and deepening our understanding.

How we synthesize our experiences shapes the way we perceive and interact with the world. This is why journaling has proven to be a powerful therapeutic tool in treating people who suffer from trauma or mental illness. Expressive writing, for example, helps us process painful experiences by externalizing them through long-form journaling. Cognitive behavioral therapy (CBT) uses scripts to treat people obsessing over intrusive thoughts. A distressing thought is detailed in a short paragraph. This script is then written over and over again until the thought begins to lose its death grip on the person's mind, granting some much-needed perspective and distance—something we all struggle to find when dealing with challenging situations.

Toward our latter days, writing can help preserve our most cherished memories. Studies suggest that the act of writing keeps our minds sharper for longer. I've received many emails over the years praising Bullet Journal for helping those with poor memories stay organized, regardless of age. For instance, Bridget Bradley, a fifty-one-year-old Bullet Journalist, now remembers "what the weather was like three months ago, how many times I went to the gym last month, that I have made a reservation (by email) for that restaurant table, that I am going on holiday in July, and that I have already worked out what I need to take with me (six months in advance!) so that I have time to buy and prepare for it." Similarly, I've heard from numerous people who found that Bullet Journaling helped their memory improve after being compromised by trauma or medical procedures.

A dear friend of mine once told me, "The long way *is* the short way." In a cut-and-paste world that celebrates speed, we often mistake convenience for efficiency. When we take shortcuts, we forfeit opportunities to slow down and think. Writing by hand, as nostalgic and antiquated as it may seem, allows us to reclaim that opportunity. As we craft our letters, we automatically start filtering the signal from the noise. True efficiency is not about speed; it's about spending more time with what truly matters. In the end, that's what the Bullet Journal method is all about.

II

THE SYSTEM

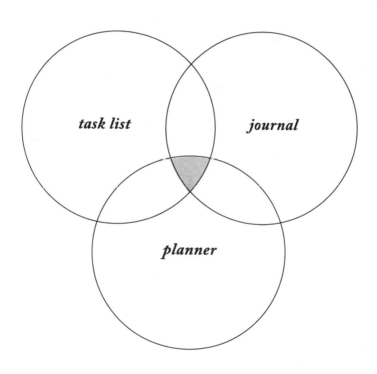

THE SYSTEM

Your Bullet Journal can be your to-do list, journal, planner, sketchbook, or all of the above, all in one place. This flexibility stems from its modular structure. An easy way to conceptualize the system is to imagine the pieces of a Lego set. Each piece of the Bullet Journal's system serves a specific function, be it ordering your day, planning your month, or tackling a goal. You're free to mix and match the pieces to customize the system to meet your needs. As those needs inevitably change over time, this flexibility allows the system to adapt and remain relevant through the different seasons of your life. As you evolve, so will the function and structure of your Bullet Journal.

In this part of the book, we'll examine the core building blocks that lay the foundation of the system. You'll learn how they work, why they work, and how they snap into the larger framework. If you're following along in sequence, here's where you'll learn how to set up your own Bullet Journal and migrate the content from your Mental Inventory.

If you're an old hand at this, Part II aims to take your BuJoJitsu to the next level. We'll delve into the tools and techniques you've been using and explore the reasoning behind their design. This section functions both as a reference and a guide to help answer any questions that may have bubbled up during your time Bullet Journaling.

If you're new to the Bullet Journal, I suggest reading through all the chapters in this part before setting pen to paper. Each method and technique is effective on its own, but the true power of the Bullet Journal is found in the sum of its parts. To get the most out of your BuJo experience, it's important to understand how these parts interact and influence each other. This part will walk you through each step, how it works, and how to set up your own Bullet Journal step by step.

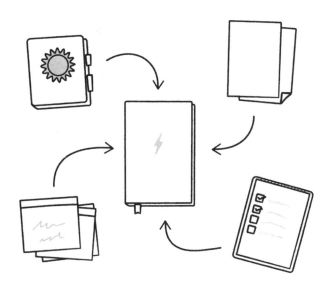

Before We Dive In . . .

Most of the organizational methods people tried to shove down my throat didn't make sense, felt impractical, and left me feeling frustrated and/or demoralized. Those are the last things I want you to feel!

I've done my best to avoid making this part read like stereo instructions, but it's unavoidably technical. At first glance, it may look like there are a lot of moving parts. As you read through the following chapters, I invite you to consider each component individually. Hold it up to the light; examine it. Ask yourself: *Would this help me?*

If at some point you feel overwhelmed, take a step back and start by implementing only the pieces that make sense. Most components are self-contained by design, so you can effectively use them even if you don't use the rest. Start with what speaks to you— even if it's just one piece—and build from there. This is also the way the Bullet Journal was born: one workable piece at a time.

KEY CONCEPTS

INDEX

Used to locate your content in your Bullet Journal using Topics and page numbers.

INDEX	INDEX
Future Log: 5-8	
Jan: 9-	
Gym Log: 13-16	
1	2

FUTURE LOG

Used to store Future Tasks and Events that fall outside the current month.

FUTURE LOG	FUTURE LOG
Feb	May
Mar	Jun
Apr	Jul
5	6

MONTHLY LOG

Provides an overview of time and tasks for the current month. Also functions as your monthly mental inventory.

JANUARY	JANUARY
1M	• Donate Clothes
2T	• Plan Trip
3W	• Back up site
4T	• Dentist
5F	• Daycare
6S	
7S	
9	10

DAILY LOG

Serves as your catchall for Rapid Logging your thoughts throughout each day

01.01.MO	01.02.TU
• Donate Clothes	• Tim: call
o Promoted!	• Yoga: cancel
X Back up site	– office closed Fri.
– Jen in town tmr	o Brit's party
• Book daycare	
11	12

KEY CONCEPTS

RAPID LOGGING

Using short-form notation paired with symbols to quickly capture, categorize, and prioritize your thoughts into Notes, Events, and Tasks.

- Note
O Event
• Task
X Task Complete
> Task Migrated
< Task Scheduled
~~• Task Irrelevant~~

COLLECTIONS

The modular building blocks of BuJo, used to store related content.
The core collections are the Index, Future Log, Monthly Log, and Daily Log, but you can create one for anything you want to keep track of.

INDEX	FUTURE LOG
MONTHLY LOG	DAILY LOG

MIGRATION

The monthly process of filtering out meaningless content from your notebook.

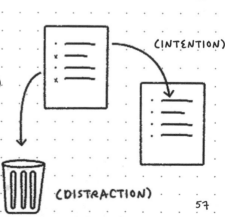

(INTENTION)

(DISTRACTION)

RAPID LOGGING

Quick—what was the last meaningful thing someone said to you? Okay, let's try an easier category: What did you eat for lunch two days ago? If you're drawing a blank, you're not alone. It goes to show that we can't rely on memory to accurately capture our experience.

Our experiences—both sweet and sour—are lessons. We honor these lessons by writing them down so we can study them and see what they have to teach us. This is how we learn, this is how we grow. If we forfeit the opportunity to learn from our experiences, as the saying (sort of) goes, we condemn ourselves to repeat our mistakes.

Journaling provides a powerful way of facilitating this path of self-learning. The problem with traditional journaling is that it is loosely structured and time-intensive. Rapid Logging leverages the best aspects of journaling by stripping away everything that's not essential. It's the language the Bullet Journal is written in. In short, Rapid Logging helps us capture and organize our thoughts as living lists.

*Rapid Logging will help you efficiently capture your
life as it happens so that you may begin to study it.*

On the following pages you'll find visual examples illustrating the difference between content captured in a more traditional way and the *same information* organized with Rapid Logging. We'll break down the symbols and structure in detail later, but it's easy to see how succinct and clear the Rapid Log is. This streamlined approach to recording our thoughts saves a lot of time, allowing it to easily fit into our busy lives.

As Bullet Journalist Ray Cheshire describes: "I'm a high school science teacher at a big inner-city school in the UK. Things can get a little hectic at times as we try to cram ever more stuff into our days. This is where Rapid Logging comes in. For example, we were told that an inspection was going to happen at very short notice, but thanks to Bullet Journaling, I quickly knew what I still had to do before the inspectors arrived."

Be it at home, school, or the workplace, Rapid Logging will help you organize the dizzying array of things you have to contend with on a daily basis.

TRADITIONAL

- [x] Call Keith back to figure out where we should eat this weekend.

- [ ] Email Heather again regarding the Acme Co release forms for project participants. Need to send out the forms to them and have their signatures before we proceed.

The Acme Co UX presentation is due February 12.

- [ ] ~~Email Leigh about her party that she's having on April 21.~~

The office will be closed on the 13th.

I was happily surprised that Margaret seems to have taken her feedback to heart. She volunteered to help manage the assets for the project and has become a more engaged part of the team. Her work is also showing progress.

- [ ] Call to cancel yoga orientation.

- [ ] Order Kim a birthday cake for next week on Thursday. It has to be gluten-free because she is celiac.

- [ ] Add hours for Acme Co project to the time tracker.

Broadway was blocked on my way to work this morning, so I had to take a detour. On the way I spotted a new coffee shop I have to try. It's also a lot more scenic a route. I put the windows down and just enjoyed the ride. I get so caught up in rushing to work that I totally forgot about this route. By the time I got to work, I was feeling pretty good even though I was a little late.

- [ ] Plan trip

---

225 words

RAPID LOGGING

04.01.TH

- Keith: Call re: Saturday dinner
- * Acme Co: Release forms
  - Heather: Email to get forms
  - > Email forms to participants
  - < Get signatures
- — Acme Co: UX presentation Feb 12
- • ~~Leigh: Reply Apr 21 party~~
- — Office closed Apr 13
- o Margaret: Volunteered to help with assets
  - — Showing more incentive and engagement
  - — Increased participation effort

04.02.FR

- x Cancel yoga
- • Kim: Get birthday cake
  - — Celiac: Needs to be gluten-free
  - — The party's on Thursday
- * Acme Co: Log hours
- o Broadway blocked, had to take long way
  - — Found new coffee place
  - — Much prettier drive
  - — Felt more relaxed when I arrived
- • Plan trip

TOPICS AND PAGINATION

The first step in Rapid Logging is to frame the content you're about to log. You do this by giving your page a Topic name. It can be as simple as "Shopping List." Even here—as with most things BuJo—there is more than meets the eye. Topics actually serve three functions:

1. They identify and describe content.
2. They serve as an opportunity for you to clarify your intention.
3. They set the agenda for the content.

How many meetings have you sat through that have little to no agenda? Generally, they're not very productive. Pausing to define the agenda *before* you start allows you to focus, prioritize, and use your time far more effectively.

Giving your page its Topic provides that opportunity to pause. What will you capture in this space? What's its purpose? What value will it add to your life? These may seem like superfluous considerations, but I can't tell you how many times I've sat down to make yet another list, only to realize that it simply wouldn't add anything meaningful to my life. Does tracking the TV shows I've watched this year add any real value? No. I can reinvest that time I saved into something that does. Other times, that pause has helped me refine my aims, keeping the content of my Bullet Journal focused and relevant. Topic by Topic, pause by pause, we're honing our ability to focus on what matters.

Often all it takes to live intentionally
is to pause before you proceed.

Lastly, a good Topic turns your Bullet Journal into a more useful reference. Who knows when you may need to look back through your journal to find a specific Topic? "Oct 13, Meeting 4 notes" says little, whereas "10.13.TH (month/date/day) / Acme Co. (client name) / Website Relaunch (project name) / User Feedback (meeting priority)" provides you with a useful description.

Once you've defined your Topic, write it at the top of the page. Now you've laid the foundation for what you want to build, but you can't locate a building without its address. That address in your Bullet Journal is the page number, so be sure to add them as you go. Page numbers will be critical when we get to Indexing (page 99). Spoiler alert: Your Index helps you quickly locate your content.

The only time we don't use a descriptive Topic is for our Daily Log (page 86). It's a catchall for our thoughts, so the daily Topic is simply the date, formatted as month/date/day. This will help you quickly orient yourself when flipping through your pages.

All this is more complicated to explain than it is to do. In practice, you're just taking a few seconds to think before putting pen to paper. Now, with the Topic and page number in place, your page is prepared to handle anything you throw at it.

04.01.TH

- Keith: Call re: Saturday dinner
- Acme Co: Release forms
  - Heather: Email to get forms
  - Email forms to participants
  - Get signatures
- Acme Co: UX presentation — Feb 12
- ~~Leigh: Reply Apr 21 party~~
- Office closed Apr 13
- ○ Margaret: Volunteered to help with assets
  - Showing more incentive and engagement
  - Increased participation effort

04.02.FR

- Cancel yoga
- Kim: Get birthday cake
  - Celiac: Needs to be gluten-free
  - The party's on Thursday
- Acme Co: Log hours
- ○ Broadway blocked, had to take long way
  - Found new coffee place
  - Much prettier drive
  - Felt more relaxed when I arrived
- Plan trip

Don't forget to number your pages!

64

BULLETS

I f Rapid Logging is the language the Bullet Journal is written in, Bullets are the syntax. Once you've set up your Topic and page number, you capture your thoughts as short, objective sentences known as Bullets. Each Bullet is paired with a specific symbol to categorize your entry. We use Bullets not only because it takes less time, but also because wrestling information into short sentences forces us to distill what's most valuable.

Crafting effective Bullets requires striking a balance between brevity and clarity. If an entry is too short, we may not be able to decipher it later. If it's too long, then writing down your thoughts becomes a chore. For example, "Return call ASAP!" is too short. Who are you calling back? What are you calling them back about? It's easy to forget all that in the rush of the day. Conversely, "Call John M. back as soon as you can because he needs to know when you will have the sales figures for June ready for him" is an overly informative word salad. Let's try again: "Call John M, re: June sales figures." You're saying exactly the same thing using only a quarter of the words. In a bit, I'll also show you how to turn that Task into a priority using Signifiers (page 80).

Keeping your entries short without losing meaning takes practice, but over time it hones our ability to identify what's worth writing down. That's important because our lives are infinitely complex, and there is potentially *a lot* to keep track of. If you've kept lists in the past, you're familiar with how quickly they can spiral out of control. They often lack context and priority. Rapid Logging solves this issue in a few ways, first by categorizing entries into:

1. Things that you need to do (Tasks)
2. Your experiences (Events)
3. Information you don't want to forget (Notes)

Each category is assigned a symbol to upgrade a basic list with much-needed additional layers of context and function. During the day, these symbols allow you to quickly capture and contextualize your thoughts in real time. Later on, they make locating specific content much easier as you scan through your pages. Let's take a look at each category and see how this syntax can keep your entries organized, lean, and effective.

TASKS

The Task bullet does a lot of heavy lifting. Think of it as a checkbox. (Older versions of the Bullet Journal used an actual checkbox, but eventually it became clear that checkboxes weren't as efficient as the dot Bullet: They take more time to draw and can look sloppy, decreasing legibility.) The Task "•" bullet is fast, clean, and flexible. It can easily be transformed into other shapes, which is important, because Tasks can have five different states:

• **Tasks:**
   Entries that require you to take action.

x **Completed Tasks:**
   Action has been completed.

➤ **Migrated Tasks:**
   Tasks that have been moved *forward* (hence the right arrow) into your next Monthly Log (page 90) or into a specific Collection (page 84).

❮ **Scheduled Tasks:**
   A Task tied to a date that falls outside of the current month and is therefore moved *backward* (hence the left arrow) into the Future Log (page 95) at the front of your book.

- ~~Irrelevant Tasks:~~

Sometimes the things we task ourselves with end up not mattering anymore. Their meaning simply expires or circumstances change. If it no longer matters, then it's a distraction. Strike it off your list. One less thing to worry about.

Subtasks and Master Tasks

Some Tasks require multiple steps to complete. These dependencies—or Subtasks—can be listed by simply indenting them directly below their Master Task. Master Tasks can only be marked as complete once all of the Subtasks have also been completed or marked as irrelevant.

TIP: When you notice a Master Task spawning a lot of Subtasks, it can indicate that this Task is growing into a project. If that's the case, you may want to turn this nested list into its own Collection (page 84). Planning a trip, for example, can be complex, with Tasks ranging from researching locations to arranging transportation—each of which might have Subtasks (check out X, Y, and Z hotels online; price flights and rent a car). If you notice that a Task is turning into a project, but you don't have time at that moment to set up a new Collection, just log a Task to remind you to set one up later: "• Create Hawaii Vacation Collection." This is a perfect example of how Bullets can serve as mental anchors.

04.01.TH

- ✗ Keith: Call re: Saturday Dinner
- • Acme Co: Release forms
  - • Heather: Email to get forms
  - \> Email forms to participants
  - \< Get signatures
- – Acme Co: UX presentation Feb 12
- • ~~Leigh: Reply Apr 21 party~~
- – Office closed Apr 13
- ○ Margaret: Volunteered to help with assets
  - – Showing more incentive and engagement
  - – Increased participation effort

04.02.FR

- ✗ Cancel yoga
- • Kim: Get birthday cake
  - – Celiac: Needs to be gluten-free
  - – The party's on Thursday
- • Acme Co: Log hours
- ○ Broadway blocked, had to take long way
  - – Found new coffee place
  - – Much prettier drive
  - – Felt more relaxed when I arrived
- • Plan trip

Writing down Tasks serves a dual purpose. First, having a record of an open task makes it easier to remember even when you're away from your journal, partly due to a phenomenon known as the Zeigarnik effect. Russian psychiatrist and psychologist Bluma Wulfovna Zeigarnik observed that the staff at her local restaurant was able to remember complex unfilled orders until they were filled, at which point they forgot the details. The friction of an unfinished Task actively engages your mind. Second, by logging Tasks and their state, you'll also automatically create an archive of your actions. This becomes immensely valuable during Reflection (page 131), or when you review your notebook days, months, or years from now. You'll always know what you were working toward.

EVENTS

Events—represented by the "o" bullet—are experience-related entries that can either be scheduled preemptively (for example, "Charlie's birthday party") or logged after they occur (for example, "Signed the lease. Yay!").

Event entries, no matter how personal or emotionally taxing, should remain as objective and brief as possible. The Event "Movie night" bears no more or less weight than "He dumped me." Not having to articulate the complexity of an experience makes it much more likely for us to write it down. That's the most important part: to have a record.

After a painful event, trying to explain how you feel in the moment can be exceptionally challenging, if not outright impossible. A joyful event can bring complex feelings, too—everything from gratitude to triumph to tears because a special loved one wasn't there to share it. In both cases, they can be overwhelming and distracting. Event bullets allow you to put a pin in an experience, to temporarily offload it from your mind, so you can refocus on other priorities. This way you have a record safely stored in your journal, ready for you to revisit whenever you have more time, perspective, or wherewithal to sort out your emotional bureaucracy.

04.01.TH

- ✗ Keith: Call re: Saturday dinner
- • Acme Co: Release forms
  - • Heather: Email to get forms
  - ❯ Email forms to participants
  - ❮ Get signatures
- − Acme Co: UX presentation Feb 12
- ~~Leigh: Reply Apr 21 party~~
- − Office closed Apr 13
- ○ Margaret: Volunteered to help with assets
  - − Showing more incentive and engagement
  - − Increased participation effort

04.02.FR

- ✗ Cancel yoga
- • Kim: Get birthday cake
  - − Celiac: Needs to be gluten-free
  - − The party's on Thursday
- • Acme Co: Log hours
- ○ Broadway blocked, had to take long way
  - − Found new coffee place
  - − Much prettier drive
  - − Felt more relaxed when I arrived
- • Plan trip

72

Take, for example, Michael S., who met a woman who he was quite taken with. It was only a few months into the relationship, and everything seemed to indicate a strong bond and bright future. One day she invited him out to dinner. Sitting there, he could tell something was off, so he asked her what was going on. She told him that she no longer wanted to see him. Blindsided, he asked why. She didn't know, but it was over.

Michael was left tormented by the confusing loss of something he believed to be potentially rare and special. A few weeks later, he picked up his Bullet Journal, which held the full record of their relationship, and leafed through their history one page at a time. He was shocked to discover that at no point during the rather brief relationship had things been nearly as good as he remembered. Entry after entry painted a picture of a rather distant person who was never particularly kind to him. The reality of the situation, penned in his own words, provided the perspective he needed to move on.

It was an important moment of clarity that enabled this Bullet Journalist to gain valuable insight that would not have been available to him otherwise. This is just one example of how having an objective account of your experience can be a powerful tool in helping you move through life. BuJo is not all about highlighting the doom and gloom, though; it can make you mindful of positives, too. We may finish our year feeling that not much of note really happened—maybe we didn't take that big Hawaii trip or get the promotion we'd hoped for, or maybe we thought we'd be further along in our apartment hunt than we are. We're all programmed with a negativity bias. Leafing through our Bullet Journal can help correct this perspective: There were celebrations, projects completed, fitness milestones achieved, clean bills of health conferred, children and pets doing adorable things, soulful talks with friends, kids, parents, or spouses, and on and on.

Our memories are unreliable. We often trick ourselves into believing things about our experiences that are biased and inaccurate. Studies suggest that our recollection of how we felt can greatly differ from the way an experience actually made us feel. We can remember wonderful events in a negative way, and negative events in a positive way. Harvard psychologist Dan Gilbert likens our memories to painted portraits instead of photographs, where our mind artistically interprets memory.[20]

It's important to keep an accurate record of how things actually happened, because we often make decisions based on our past experiences. If we operate entirely on memory, we're apt to repeat our mistakes by fooling ourselves into believing that something had an effect it actually did not. Good or bad, big or small, jot it down. Over the days, months, and years, they will form a pretty accurate roadmap of your life. Understanding how we got to where we are today will allow us to make more informed decisions as we plot our course forward.

TIP: I recommend unpacking experiences as soon as possible after the Event, so the details are fresh and accurate. The Daily Reflection (page 134) works well toward this end.

TIP: Events that need to be scheduled on specific dates that fall outside of the current month are added to the Future Log (page 95). Like birthdays, meetings, and dinners.

TIP: For those of you who enjoy writing, long-form or expressive journaling (page 269), you can nest Note bullets (page 271) under an Event bullet if there are important/interesting details that you want to capture about an experience for later use. Again, keep it brief:

o   Date with Sam at El Pastor
  – She was 15 minutes late. Didn't text. Didn't apologize.
  – Made fun of the fact that I dressed up for the date.
  – She ordered a lot and didn't eat much. Didn't offer to pay.
  – The guac was incredible.

NOTES

Represented with the "–" dash, Notes include facts, ideas, thoughts, and observations. They log information you want to remember that isn't immediately or necessarily actionable. This type of bullet works well for meetings, lectures, and classrooms . . . we all know what notes are, so I won't belabor the point. That said, few of us are ever taught how to take them. Let's delve into the tips, tricks, and benefits of taking notes the Bullet Journal way.

By keeping your Notes short, you're forced to distill information down to the essential. The more content you try to capture during a lecture or a meeting, the less you're thinking about what's being said. You burn through most of your attention parroting the source.

Being both strategic and economical with your word choices forces you to engage your mind. By asking yourself what's important and *why*, you go from passively listening to actively *hearing* what's being said. It's when we begin to *hear* that information can transform into understanding. A main focus of Bullet Journaling is to get better at hearing the world around us as well as the one within so we can begin to understand. More of that in Part III.

04.01.TH

- x Keith: Call re: Saturday dinner
- • Acme Co: Release forms
  - • Heather: Email to get forms
  - > Email forms to participants
  - < Get signatures
- — Acme Co: UX presentation — Feb 12
- ~~Leigh: Reply Apr 21 party~~
- — Office closed Apr 13
- ° Margaret: Volunteered to help with assets
  - — Showing more incentive and engagement
  - — Increased participation effort

04.02.FR

- x Cancel yoga
- • Kim: Get birthday cake
  - — Celiac: Needs to be gluten-free
  - — The party's on Thursday
- • Acme Co: Log hours
- ° Broadway blocked, had to take long way
  - — Found new coffee place
  - — Much prettier drive
  - — Felt more relaxed when I arrived
- • Plan trip

Let It Sink In

Don't immediately bail when the meeting, class, or lecture is over. Information is contextual. When you're being exposed to new information, the story unfolds one piece at a time. It's not until the end that you'll see how the pieces fit together. Once the event is over, take a few moments and use the time to your advantage. Sit for a while and give yourself a moment to process what you heard. Capture whatever surfaces. Often you'll gain new insight when you can better contextualize the information as a whole. Take a step back, review your notes, see what else bubbles up, and write it down. This is a great opportunity to fill gaps in your understanding or highlight them. Having a list of questions can help your next interaction be far more targeted and productive. Curiosity is also a strong source of motivation, which can help facilitate proactive engagement with the content. If you really want to know something, you'll find out.

Make It Yours

Whenever possible, try to latch on to information that you can relate to, that genuinely interests you. Here is one example of how you can apply all of these tips:

> **Source:** "Some groups of animals enjoy unusual colloquial names. A group of flamingos is called a flamboyance of flamingos. A group of crows is known as a murder of crows. . . . A group of pugs is known as a grumble of pugs."

Ineffective Note: Some animal groups have names.

Effective Note: A group of pugs is called a grumble! A murder of crows!

Although the first Note is succinct, if you read it weeks from now, you might be confused, thinking the Note referred to "mammals," "reptiles," or "lagomorphs." The second bullet, on the other hand, binds the information to something you care about (in this case pugs; if you don't like pugs—you heartless monster—then maybe crows would be better) and helps you extrapolate a lot more information. If groups of pugs and crows have unusual names, then it stands to reason that other groups of animals may as well. This succinct-yet-specific Note might trigger additional recollections about the topic. You might even set up a Task to look up more information.

One simple way to summarize all these tips is this: Keep your future self in mind. Your Notes will be useless if they can't be deciphered in a week, month, or year from now. Do your future self a kindness and don't sacrifice clarity for brevity. It will keep your Bullet Journal valuable for years to come.

SIGNIFIERS AND CUSTOM BULLETS

The Task, Event, and Note bullets will serve you well in most situations. That said, everyone's needs are different. One size does not fit all. This is a core tenet of Bullet Journaling. This is why you're encouraged to customize the system once you're comfortable with the basics. We'll fully explore how to do this in Part IV, but for now, I'd like to give you a glimpse into fine-tuning your Bullet Journal to suit your needs through Signifiers and Custom Bullets.

Signifiers

Another way that Rapid Logging improves on the functionality of lists is through the use of Signifiers. These are symbols used to highlight specific entries to give them additional context. Signifiers are placed in front of bullets so they stick out from the rest of your list, making them easy for the scanning eye to locate (page 81). Here are some examples of Signifiers that I've found to be helpful:

04.01.TH

- Keith: Call re: Saturday dinner
- * • Acme Co: Release forms
  - Heather: Email to get forms
  - > Email forms to participants
  - < Get signatures
- – Acme Co: UX presentation Feb 12
- ~~Leigh: Reply Apr 21 party~~
- – Office closed Apr 13
- o Margaret: Volunteered to help with assets
  - – Showing more incentive and engagement
  - – Increased participation effort

04.02.FR

- x Cancel yoga
- Kim: Get birthday cake
  - – Celiac: Needs to be gluten-free
  - – The party's on Thursday
- * • Acme Co: Log hours
- o Broadway blocked, had to take long way
  - – Found new coffee place
  - – Much prettier drive
  - – Felt more relaxed when I arrived
- ! • Plan trip

Priority: Represented by "*" asterisk. Used to mark a bullet as important and is most commonly paired with the Task Bullet. Use this sparingly. If everything is a priority, nothing is.

Inspiration: Represented by "!" exclamation point. Most commonly paired with a Note. Great ideas, personal mantras, and genius insights will never be misplaced again!

Custom Bullets

Custom Bullets help you quickly capture entries that are unique to your situation. For example, people who delegate a lot of Tasks can add another state to the Task Bullet by turning it into a forward slash, indicating that it was assigned to someone else:

/ Presentation. @KevinB pulling numbers

When Kevin pulls the numbers, you can then just turn the "/" forward slash into an "X" to mark it as complete.

Custom Bullets are the way to go when you have recurring Tasks or Events like "Football practice." Football practice might be an "H" (because it looks like a field goal). You can quickly add this Bullet to the Calendar page in your Monthly Log (page 90), so you can see when practice is at a glance. Feel free to use letters instead of icons if they help you remember.

TIP: Keep Custom Bullets and Signifiers to an absolute minimum. Rapid Logging tries to remove as much friction as possible from capturing information. The more you invent, the more complex it is, and the slower you will become.

Rapid Logging Summary

Now we've walked through all the steps of Rapid Logging, a quick and effective way to capture and sort your thoughts into Tasks, Events, and Notes. You contain those thoughts with a Topic to help you set your intention and a page number to easily locate it again later.

Rapid Logging is designed to help you contend with the daily grind. It will allow you to offload all the information you're bombarded with and emerge from a chaotic day with a clear categorized list of prioritized thought.

COLLECTIONS

#bulletjournalcollection

No matter how organized you try to be, life is messy and often wildly unpredictable. The Bullet Journal embraces the chaos by not trying to fight it. It trades in the linear structure of traditional planners for a modular approach.

Like a Lego set, BuJo is comprised of modular blocks. Each module is a template designed to organize and collect related information; that's why we refer to them as Collections. Collections are interchangeable, reusable, and customizable. Maybe last month you created a shopping list, organized a trip, and prepared for a presentation. This month, however, you may need to create a fertility tracker, set up a party, and plan your meals. Whatever information you need to organize, there is a Collection for that. If you can't find one, you're encouraged to invent one of your own (more on that in Part IV).

The portfolio of Collections—also known as your Stack—that you choose to use is entirely up to you, and it will change over time. This makes the Bullet Journal incredibly flexible and allows it to continuously adapt to a wide variety of uses. This is also why the Bullet Journals you see online don't look similar to one another.

Each Bullet Journal reflects the unique needs of its user at that moment in time.

In the following pages you'll learn about the four core Collections: the Daily Log, the Monthly Log, the Future Log, and the one Collection to rule them all, the Index. These will serve as the foundational structure for your notebook. Let's take a closer look at each, see how they relate to one another, and explore how they can help order your chaos one piece at a time.

THE DAILY LOG

#bulletjournaldailylog

The Daily Log is the workhorse of your Bullet Journal. Its streamlined template is designed to capture your daily deluge in real time. When you're in the thick of it, you can rely on your Daily Log to keep your thoughts organized with very little effort so you can focus on the task at hand.

To set up your Daily Log, all you have to do is add the day's date and the page number. That's it! With your container in place, you're all set to Rapid Log (page 58) your Tasks, Events, and Notes as they occur throughout the day. The idea is to be consistently unburdening your mind. It will be able to rest assured, knowing that everything is safely recorded in your notebook.

Your Daily Log is more than a simple to-do list. Yes, it serves to capture your responsibilities, but it also helps you document your experiences. It's a safe place where your mind is free to express itself, judgment-free and always happy to welcome your thoughts as they bubble up throughout the day. Over time those thoughts become a record of your state of being, which becomes incredibly valuable when we get into Reflection (page 131). It provides the context we often lack in our daily lives. With context we can be more deliberate with our actions.

DAILY LOG

04.01.TH

- •   Keith: Call re: Saturday dinner
- * •   Acme Co: Release forms
  - •   Heather: Email to get forms
  - >   Email forms to participants
  - <   Get signatures
- −   Acme Co: UX presentation Feb 12
- •   ~~Leigh: Reply Apr 21 party~~
- −   Office closed Apr 13
- ○   Margaret: Volunteered to help with assets
  - −   Showing more incentive and engagement
  - −   Increased participation effort

04.02.FR

- ✕   Cancel yoga
- •   Kim: Get birthday cake
  - −   Celiac: Needs to be gluten-free
  - −   The party's on Thursday
- * •   Acme Co: Log hours
- ○   Broadway blocked, had to take long way
  - −   Found new coffee place
  - −   Much prettier drive
  - −   Felt more relaxed when I arrived!
- •   Plan trip

I've tried my hand at nearly every organizational system available. None of them stuck because they required me to invest a great deal of money or time to master their technique.

I started BuJo with a 25-cent notebook and a mechanical pencil. I find BuJo is less concerned with structure than it is with intention. I add activities and tasks to my Daily Log as the day unfolds. The day becomes more about flow, with the Bullet Journal as both monitor and log.

—Kevin D.

On Space

A common question I get is how much space the Daily Log requires. My answer: as much space as that day needs, and that's something you just can't know in advance. Some Daily Logs can span many pages, while others won't take up half a page. It's nearly impossible to tell how your day may unfold. Though it can be helpful to set an intention for the day, like *Today I will not complain*, it's important to remember not to set an expectation for your day, because that's out of your control.

If our lives are oceans, then our days are waves; some big, some small. Your Bullet Journal is the shore, and it will be carved by both.

If you don't fill a page, add the next date wherever you left off and you're good to go. You should never feel like you're running out of room. This is why I advise against setting up your Daily Logs way ahead of time. Either create them the day of or the night before.

Once you get rolling with BuJo, your Daily Log may start to feel less like the stress-inducing to-do lists you may be accustomed to and more like a record and a reminder to live according to your intentions, one day at a time.

THE MONTHLY LOG

#bulletjournalmonthlylog

T his Collection helps you step back and take a breath before diving into the coming month. It offers a bird's-eye view of the things you have to do, as well as your available time. If each Bullet Journal is another volume in the story of your life, then the Monthly Log marks a new chapter. They're small but significant milestones punctuating the year. Setting them up allows us to regularly check in with ourselves so that we can maintain/regain context, motivation, and focus.

The Monthly Log is set up on a spread of facing pages. The left page will be your Calendar page; the right page will be your Tasks page. The Topic of this Collection is the name of the month, and we add it to both pages of the spread (pages 91–92).

Calendar Page

On the Calendar page, list the dates of that month down the left edge of the page, followed by the first letter of the corresponding

(CALENDAR PAGE)

FEBRUARY

1	M	Sent out newsletter. 172.5 lbs—down 5!
2	T	
3	W	Dinner Michael @ Faro
4	T	
5	F	Becca goodbye dinner @ Walters
6	S	Tara Brach seminar @ Omega
7	S	
8	M	
9	T	Mailed out tax forms
10	W	
11	T	Acme Co contract signed
12	F	
13	S	
* 14	S	Game Chem Co. preso. Went well!
15	M	
16	T	Jenna birthday dinner @ Ichiran
17	W	
* 18	T	Lost heat. Lost Redrum project :(
19	F	
20	S	
21	S	
22	M	Heat restored
* 23	T	Launch Sokura website!
24	W	
25	T	
26	F	
27	S	
28	S	

(TASKS PAGE)

FEBRUARY

- Steph: Dry ice delivery
- Cancel yoga orientation
- Get Kim birthday cake!
- Log hours
- Submit expenses
- Send Linda vacation photos
- Pay rent
- Call Grandma
- Drop off laundry
- Schedule doctor's appointment
- Buy dress for Vivian's wedding
- Make playlist for Vivian's wedding

day of the week (page 91). Remember to leave some room in the left margin so you can add Signifiers later, if needed. Signifiers will allow you to quickly scan your Calendar page to find anything particularly noteworthy.

Feel free to use this page like a traditional calendar, by slotting in your Events and Tasks ahead of time. That said, nothing is set in stone, so I prefer to log Events only *after* they happen. That way, the Monthly Log's Calendar page acts like a timeline.

This timeline is something your future self will often be grateful for, as it can provide a lot of clarity and context—it shows you exactly what you focused on in a given month by highlighting precisely when it actually happened.

TIP: Keep your entries as short as possible, as the Monthly Log is designed for reference only.

TIP: For some added clarity, you can add lines dividing the weeks.

Tasks Page (or Mental Inventory)

The Tasks page of your Monthly Log will serve as your ongoing Mental Inventory page. Give yourself permission to sit for as long as it takes to offload the action items that have been swimming around your head. What matters this month? What are the priorities?

When you're done capturing your thoughts, go through the previous month and see what Tasks remain open. Transfer any important items into the new Monthly Log's Tasks page. We'll delve deeper into this process in the chapter on Migration (page 107), but for now, just know this is how Tasks don't slip through the cracks when you Bullet Journal. We rewrite things until we get them done or they become irrelevant.

THE FUTURE LOG

#bulletjournalfuturelog

The Bullet Journal unfolds organically based on what you need in the here and now, so you may be wondering how you can plan for the future. For this we use a Collection known as the Future Log. The Future Log stores entries that have specific dates that fall outside of the current month. So if it's September, and you've got a project with a deadline of, say, December 15, *shwoooops*, into the Future Log it goes.

The Future Log lives at the front of your Bullet Journal, right after your Index (page 99). It usually requires 1–2 spreads of facing pages and can be designed in many different ways. I've included a lean yet effective three-month example (page 97).

So how does this work in practice? During the day, just continue to write everything down in your Daily Log (page 86), even future Tasks. Again, the Daily Log is there to prevent us from having to waste time thinking about where to write things down. It's a catch-all, designed to hold our thoughts until we're ready to sort them out. When that time comes—like during Daily Reflection (page 134)—you'll transfer any bullets with a future date *from* your Daily Log *into* your Future Log. Once you do, be sure to mark the entry as scheduled "<" in your Daily Log. This way you will know that it's been addressed, so you can temporarily offload it from your mind.

Think of the Future Log as a queue, each item eagerly waiting for its month to arrive. When you're setting up a new Monthly Log (page 90), be sure to scan your Future Log for any items in the queue that are ready now. If so, migrate (page 107) those items *from* your Future Log *into* your Monthly Log's Tasks page. Be sure to mark it as migrated in your Future Log.

FUTURE LOG CYCLE

" • Acme: Site Presentation December 23 "

Daily Logs (October) → Reflection → Future Log → Migration → Monthly Log (December)

FUTURE LOG

OCT

- ○ 6-7   Design Conference: NYC
- • 16   Maya: Dinner

NOV

- • 3   James Co: Paperwork due
- • 14   Venton Vision: Submit outline
- ○ 9-11 San Diego trip

DEC

- ○ 11   Jonathan's birthday
- * • 15   Yay tea: Site presentation

Once you get the hang of it, it becomes an effective way of keeping you aware of the responsibilities you're putting into your life. Your Future Log functions as a time machine that reveals the outline of the future you're building, so you can course correct if necessary.

THE INDEX

#bulletjournalindex

I've always kept a work journal where I entered telephone conversations, meeting notes, and other details of my workday chronologically. I also had a gazillion to-do lists and sticky notes, a paper calendar on my desk, and, eventually, an electronic calendar on my phone.

Whenever I needed to retrieve any notes from my work journal, I'd first have to hunt in my calendars for the date of the meeting or phone call—or guess at when it might have happened. Then I'd have to flip through my journals to find the date I was looking for.

The Bullet Journal system was an awesome refinement to my chronological system. All I do now is go to my Index, where I've written the page number of what I'm seeking, and then flip right to it!

—Cheryl S. Bridges

Your Bullet Journal notebook welcomes any part of you that you're willing to share. One moment you're planning your week; the next, sketching out a room layout or penning a poem. While getting lost in your notebook can be a lovely and liberating experience, losing things *in* your notebook decidedly is not. At this point in the book you may be wondering how you will keep track of all these different Collections. In the Bullet Journal, we solve this challenge with our Index.

The Index provides an easy way to find
your thoughts days, months, or years after
entrusting them to your notebook.

Part table of contents, part traditional index, the Index lives on the very first pages of your notebook. You can think of the Index as a container that stores all of your other Collections (except for your Daily Log, for reasons I'll explain later).

I recommend allocating two spreads—four facing pages—for your Index (if you own the official Bullet Journal notebook, the Index is already included). To add a Collection to your Index, simply write down the Collection's Topic and page numbers (page 101).

As you see in the example, Collections don't need to be consecutive. Life is unpredictable and it often requires us to shift gears, to focus on new priorities. The Index makes it easy to shift between priorities at will. If you want to resume using a previous Collection, but you're out of pages in the original instance, simply flip to the next blank spread and continue the same Topic. Then all you need to do is add the page number of this new instance back to your Index as in the following example.

INDEX

Does not need to be consecutive.

Subcollections

When you're working on a project with a lot of moving parts, each of those parts deserves its own separate Subcollection. As you can see in the example on page 101, "User Behavior Project" has four Subcollections, each dedicated to a different part of the project.

Dedicated Index

Some Bullet Journals focus on very specific subject matter. If you're a student, it could be your current curriculum. If you're a project manager, it could be for keeping track of all the different parts of your project(s). In these cases, you can use an alternate approach known as the Dedicated Index. It works much the same way as the standard Index, except that each Index page is dedicated to one subject only.

So if you were taking classes in science, English, math, and history, you would set up an Index page for each. For example, if you were taking a class in American History, one page in your Index would have the Topic "American History." Each section of the course would define a Master Collection, and each subject *within* the section would be the Subcollection.

AMERICAN HISTORY (INDEX PAGE)

Revolutionary Wars: (Master Collection)
    Battle of Lexington: 10–14
    Battle of Fort Ticonderoga: 15–20   (Subcollections)
    Battle of Bunker Hill: 21–32

NEW ACME CO SITE

Brainstorm: 10–15

Site Design:
    User flows: 16–26
    User flow / review / 0419: 27–28
    Wireframes: 29–40
    Wireframe / review 1 / 0425: 41–43
    Wireframe / review 2 / 0501: 44–46
    Design: 47–52
    Design / review 1 / 0510: 53–54
    Design / review 2 / 0515: 55–57
    User testing: 58–61, 63, 65

Site Content:
    Content strategy: 70–75
    Updated bios / and section descriptions: 76–83, 99
    Product descriptions: 84–85, 92–94

Dedicated Indexes are not limited to the classroom. Here's
an example of how it could be used to launch a new company
website.

Threading

Though the Index is an effective way to help you navigate your notebook, some of you may be thinking that there seems to be a lot of flipping about going on. There's a solution for this: threading.

This technique was brought to me by software engineer and Bullet Journal community member Carey Barnett. It quickly found a permanent home in my own practice (I love it when that happens!). Threading is used in code to point one piece of code toward a related piece of code. In the Bullet Journal, we use the same concept to point to previous or later instances of related content within our notebook.

So let's say you have a Collection (instance 1) that you started on pages 10–15. Time goes by, and you have to shift your focus to other things. You use up pages in your notebook. When you want to resume your previous Collection, you create another instance (instance 2) on pages 51–52. You shift gears again for a while, and then you continue the Collection on pages 160–170 (instance 3).

To thread these instances together, all you have to do is add the page number of one instance next to the page numbers of the other instances. So if you're at the start of instance 2, you would write "10" next to page 51 (threading back to instance 1, which is on pages 10–15). At the end of instance 2, next to page 52, you would write "160," threading forward to instance 3 (on pages 160–170). Now you can quickly flip between instances without using your Index.

THREADING

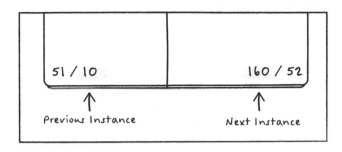

This technique has since been further expanded by community member Kim Alvarez to work with threading entire notebooks! If you wanted to continue a Collection, say, "Books to Read," in a new notebook, but you don't want to copy everything over, you can thread it. If the first instance of the "Books to Read" Collection is on page 34 in your second Bullet Journal, you would write "2.34" next to the page number in your new notebook's "Books to Read" Collection. Here the "2" indicates the volume number of your Bullet Journal and "34" represents the page number of the Collection in that volume.

This notation also makes it easy for you to add threaded notebooks to your Index. If you want to add content from a previous notebook to your new notebook, all you have to do is add it to your Index like this: **Books to Read: (2.34), 13.**

Over time your Index will double as a "table of context." It provides you with a bird's-eye view of how you're investing your time and energy. It's a map of all the things you're saying yes to. Remember, for everything you say yes to, you're also saying no to something else. Yes means work, it means sacrifice, it means investing time into one thing that you can no longer invest into another.

Use your Index to help you stay focused on the things that are worthy of your yes.

MIGRATION

There is nothing quite so useless as doing with great efficiency something that should not be done at all.

—PETER DRUCKER

There are a lot of productivity systems that help us create lists, but few encourage us to reengage with them. By hoarding tasks, our lists quickly become endless and unmanageable, leaving us feeling overwhelmed or demotivated. It's easy to forget that just because something *could* be done does not mean that it *should* be done.

Productivity is about getting more done by working on fewer things.

We need to be vigilant about regularly curating our commitments so that we can focus our time and energy on things that actually matter. In BuJo, Migration helps us form this habit.

During Migration, we transfer content from one place in our

Bullet Journal to another by rewriting it. This may seem like a lot of effort, but it serves a critical purpose: It weeds out distractions. Because it takes a little bit more time to rewrite things by hand, there's a built-in incentive to pause and consider each candidate. If an entry isn't worth the few seconds of effort required to rewrite it, then it's probably not that important. Get rid of it. Do you really need to go to that event, run that errand, host that party, file that report? Sometimes you do, but oftentimes you don't.

We pick up a lot of stowaways during the daily hustle. It's easier to just accept tasks than it is to carefully evaluate them in the moment. This is how empty responsibilities quickly accumulate, leaching your mental resources for as long as you let them. By rewriting your tasks, you have the opportunity to vet your responsibilities and throw the useless ones overboard. Simply put, Migration keeps you from operating on autopilot, wasting tremendous amounts of time working on things that don't add value to your life.

Monthly Migration

The main Migration happens at the end of every month, when you're ready to set up a new Monthly Log (page 90). In the last couple days of April, for example, you'd set up your new Monthly Log for May. Once that's done, slowly scan all of the pages of the past month, reviewing the state of your Tasks. Chances are you haven't completed them all. *This is totally normal.* Transform any guilt into curiosity by asking yourself *why* each Task might still be incomplete. Does it matter? Is it vital? What would happen if you didn't do it?

If you realize an incomplete Task has become irrelevant, strike it out. Take a moment to enjoy the feeling of having reclaimed a portion of your time. Give yourself some credit; this is a win! All wins—no matter how small—should merit at least a moment of appreciation.

If a Task remains relevant, if it still adds value to your life, then migrate it. You can migrate an item in three different ways:

1. Transcribe the open Task to the Tasks page of your new Monthly Log (page 90). Then mark the old entry as migrated ">".
2. Transcribe the Task into a Custom Collection (page 237). Then mark the old entry as migrated ">".
3. If the Task is date-specific and falls outside of the current month—migrate it into your Future Log (page 95). Then mark it as scheduled "<".

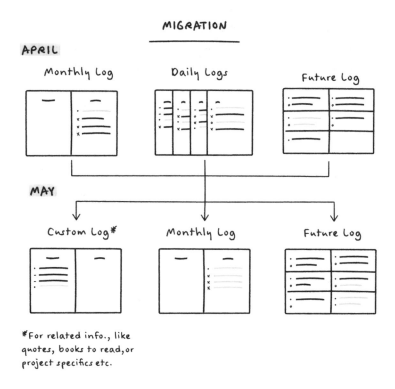

*For related info., like
quotes, books to read, or
project specifics etc.

TIP: When setting up your new Monthly Log, be sure to check your Future Log. Are any tasks or events queued up for the coming month? If so, migrate those entries *from* your Future Log *into* your new Monthly Log's Tasks or Calendar page.

TIP: If you're new to Bullet Journaling, your first Monthly Migration can be a real lightbulb moment. This is where it all begins to click. That's why I highly encourage new Bullet Journalists to stick with Bullet Journaling for at least two to three months when testing it out.

Yearly/Notebook Migration

At the beginning of every year, no matter where you are in your current BuJo notebook, start a new one. This may seem wasteful, but christening a new journal at the right time can be very empowering and motivational. The new year is as good a time as any to set up a new notebook, because it's an unavoidable cultural milestone, both literally and metaphorically. It delineates the old from the new, what has been from what could be. Why not welcome this opportunity for a fresh start? It gives us an excuse to drop any useless baggage weighing us down, lightening our load for the new adventures to come.

When you get to the end of a notebook, or a year, review your Index. Take stock of all the Collections that you've accumulated. There you'll find a fairly accurate account of how you've been spending your time and energy. Now's the time to make the hard call. Do these Collections (and their open Tasks) get to accompany you into your next Bullet Journal?

We honor the lessons we've learned by applying them to the next phase of our life. Big or small, migrate only the content and techniques that have *proven* themselves to be valuable, nothing else. A new notebook is not about starting over—it's about leveling up.

Migrating notebooks is a benevolent reckoning, where you face your responsibilities to see what they've given you and what they've taken away. Take a hard look at your journal, because there you'll see your story unfolding, written in your own hand. Each Bullet

Journal becomes another volume in the story of your life. Does it represent the life you want to live? If not, then leverage the lessons you've learned to change the narrative in the next volume.

TIP: Weekly Log (#bulletjournalweeklylog): Some Bullet Journalists like to migrate Bullets on a weekly rather than a monthly cycle. I use Weekly Logs only when I have *a lot* on my plate. I'm not wild about rewriting things either, so I only do it when it helps me stay on top of my game. Others find weekly migration useful when they *don't* have a lot going on, and they can fit a whole week's worth of Tasks on a page or two. Again, it always depends on what suits your needs. I like to keep my Weekly Log simple, so I repurpose the Daily Log template, except the Topic is the week's date range—say, "June 14–21."

Migrating Your Mental Inventory

To get a taste of Migration, you can use the Mental Inventory that you created earlier to populate your notebook. Before you dive in, review your Mental Inventory. Make sure everything you listed is worth the time and energy it will take to rewrite it; to filter out the meaningful from the meaningless.

Now decide what things you need to work on over the following month. Those items will go into the Monthly Log's Tasks page. Future Tasks and Events will go into your Future Log. Related items, like books you want to read, will be organized into their own Custom Collection.

Don't worry about getting everything right or perfect. Every master starts by picking up a tool for the first time. This is just the first step in a process that will continue to evolve as long as you Bullet Journal. Be patient with yourself, and remember, do what works for *you*.

THE LETTER

Now you may be asking yourself, why would I bother doing all this stuff? It's a fair question. So before we get into the big *why* behind Bullet Journaling itself, I want to share a letter from a Bullet Journalist, who requested to remain anonymous, that exemplifies just how impactful the system can be when integrated into your life. Organization is only partly about crossing things off our list; it's also about becoming aware of what truly matters.

It's a parent's worst nightmare: standing by helplessly as your child struggles to breathe. The EMTs rush into the room with their giant bags and a stretcher, firing off stats and rapid questions to those nearby. The kid turns blue, eyes sliding shut. They start CPR, and you watch as the little body jumps with each push on his chest.

This was the scene a week ago in my son's preschool class. His eight classmates all have health and developmental problems ranging from moderate to severe, and the class exists to help them catch up with their peers. Among the ailments are brain tumors, multiple sclerosis, cystic fibrosis, autism, and cancer in remission. The little boy who stopped breathing had been acting a little funny earlier that day, but was not feverish or sick—not five minutes earlier, he was happy and playing alongside my son at the train table.

I looked away to help another kiddo find an orange crayon and then, all of a sudden, shouting and semi-controlled chaos. Then 9-1-1. Then the EMTs. Then the oxygen rushed out of the room and I think those of us parents and teachers on duty collectively held our breaths as the rest of the children were herded off to neighboring classrooms for safekeeping.

The mom on duty that day was the victim's mother. She was not calm. Her hands shook almost to the point where she bobbled her entire purse while searching through it. Tears rolled down her cheeks when the EMTs rushed in and removed her boy's hand from hers so that they could work on him. Still, she had the presence of mind to pull out a well-worn, thread-bound book that is quite familiar to me: It was an orchid-colored, soft-covered Leuchtturm1917. The elastic was pulled down over the bottom left corner, holding a pen to the spine. It was a Bullet Journal.

Grasping the last few pages, she shredded them away from the threaded spine and held them out to the EMT asking her questions. She shook her head and sobbed, "I can't . . . I can't . . ."

"I have a pulse," the other EMT announced, while the guy in charge looked over the papers in astonishment. I sat down next to the mom and put my arm around her shoulders. This could easily be my child on the floor, I thought. Any of our children in this classroom.

The mom told him shakily what was on the paper: "His dosages and meds, his specialists and file numbers, phone numbers, allergies." She sucked in a breath. "Seizure log. There's a seizure log in there," she said. I squeezed her shoulders in support; mine has seizures, too. She rattled off his birthday as they stabilized him for transportation.

The EMT just shook his head and said to her, "Thank you. This is exactly what we need to help him. I have to call this in." And he pulled out his phone to do just that, rattling off vital information to whomever he was speaking with. She rode in the ambulance with her son; I watched as they banged the back doors shut and sped off, lights and sirens at full.

I hugged my son a little harder that night and then sat down and wrote a new spread in my own journal with emergency information, medications and dosages, a seizure log, phone numbers, file numbers, and an allergy list. Over the course of this evening, I went through an entire box of tissues before I called her cell. "He's okay," she told me. "The doctor said that the info the EMTs sent ahead allowed them to act fast. He's going to be okay. He's okay," she repeated again, choked and hoarse, but I could hear the gratefulness in her voice.

My son's friend has returned to school and carries a tiny oxygen cylinder in a tiny oxygen cylinder backpack. He's adorably sad about having to carry it. But he's alive, happy, and whole, which is all a parent can really ask for their children. I've also noticed that the other parents are now carrying notebooks of their own, presumably with the vitals necessary to help their kids in them.

No one thinks that the next child in the next ambulance could be theirs, or that their elderly mother may have an emergency fall, or that after a car accident, one may not be able to remember all of the vital information needed to treat their family members safely in the hospital. But let's be honest here . . . we all know someone who has needed that information recently. We all have passed the accident on the highway. We all have had that momentary lapse in memory when asked something about our or our children's medical records. Write it down. Keep it with you. Be prepared to commit the ultimate BuJo sin and rip it out in an emergency situation. You could save a life—your own, your child's, your sister's, your father's . . . Being organized could be the difference between life and death.

SET UP YOUR BULLET JOURNAL

1: SET UP THE INDEX*

- Number pages 1-4
- Title page "Index"
- Only add things to the Index that have content! No empty Collections!

INDEX	INDEX
Future Log: 5-8 Jan: 9- Goals: 13-16	
1	2

2: SET UP THE FUTURE LOG*

- Number pages 5-8
- Divide page into 6 cells
- Label cells with next months
- Add Future Tasks and Events
- Add it to your Index

FUTURE LOG	FUTURE LOG
Feb _____	May
Mar _____	Jun _____
Apr _____	Jul
5	6

3: SET UP THE MONTHLY LOG

- Number pages 9-10
- Title pages with current month
- List dates and monthly tasks
- Add "9-" to your Index

JANUARY	JANUARY
1M	• Donate Clothes
2T	• Plan Trip
3W	• Back up site
4T	• Dentist
5F	• Daycare
6S	
7S	
9	10

4: SET UP THE DAILY LOG

- Add page number
- Add today's date as the Topic
- Write down today's Tasks
- Daily Logs don't get Indexed

01.01.MO	01.02.TU
• Donate Clothes	• Tim: call
o Promoted!	• Yoga: cancel
X Back up site	– office closed Fri.
– Jen in town tmr	o Brit's party
• Book daycare	
11	12

*Included in the official Bullet Journal notebook

USING YOUR MENTAL INVENTORY (OPTIONAL)

5: REVIEW MENTAL INVENTORY

- Cross out anything that isn't vital or important.
- Identify related content (i.e., goals, projects, shopping lists, etc.) to create Custom Collections.**

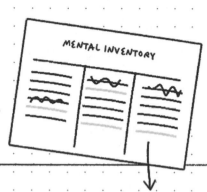

6: MIGRATE MENTAL INVENTORY

- Move Future items into the Future Log
- Migrate Items into Monthly Log
- Prioritize Monthly Log
- Migrate Priorities into your Daily Log
- Migrate any additional items into Custom Collections **

Future Log

Monthly Log

**CUSTOM COLLECTIONS

We'll cover these at length in Part IV, but they're used to store related content like goals, projects, or Focused lists. Set them up the same way (with topics and page numbers) to add them to your Index.

Daily Log

Examples Include:

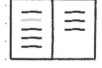

Goals

Groceries

Med Tracker

Reading List

III

THE PRACTICE

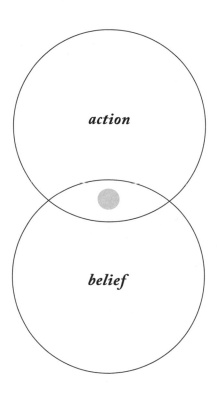

THE PRACTICE

Life is what happens to you while you're
busy making other plans.
—ALLEN SAUNDERS

Now you have all the tools you need to use your Bullet Journal to get organized. It's an important step toward assuming responsibility for the precious little time and energy that we're given. That said, organization can become a cleverly disguised form of distraction.

You can spend hours crafting to-do lists without ever crossing off a single thing. You may disappear down the rabbit hole of cleaning your house while more important projects suffer. You can spend days, months, even years working in highly organized ways toward the wrong things (as I did with my Paintapic start-up). The significance of *what* we're doing, or *how* we're doing it, pales in comparison to *why* we're doing it in the first place.

Being busy doesn't necessarily mean
we're being productive.

Being busy can be likened to tumbling down an existential staircase: stimulus, reaction, stimulus, reaction. This frenetic cycle of reactivity holds our attention hostage, limiting our ability to recognize opportunities for love, growth, and purpose. These are the things that add value to our lives, yet they're easily obscured by the rush of our busy lives.

In order to become truly productive, we must first break this cycle. We need to wedge a space between the things that happen to us and the way that we react to them. In this space, we're granted an opportunity to examine our experience. Here we can learn what's in our control, what's meaningful, what's worth our attention, and *why*. It's how we begin to define who we are and what we believe in.

Realizations like these are an important step forward, but the things we learn are simply thoughts. Like most thoughts, they fade over time, especially if they remain abstract and don't play an active role in our lives. Even the most fervent beliefs or helpful lessons can dissipate unless they're actively applied. What if you could put your beliefs into practice on a regular basis, test-driving promising ideas and measuring their impact on your life when put into action?

In Part III, you'll discover how the Bullet Journal method can serve as a bridge between your beliefs and your actions. Each chapter will explore guiding philosophies from a variety of traditions *and* teach you how to put them into practice with the help of your notebook. Step by step, we'll close the distance between *what* we're doing and *why* by defining how to live an intentional life, one that's both productive and meaningful.

KEY CONCEPTS

You can't make time, you can only take time.

Happiness is the by-product of meaning.
In order to be happy, you have to figure
out what is meaningful. You figure out what is
meaningful by putting in the time to. . . .

Cultivate your curiosity through setting goals.
We accomplish our goals by breaking them
down into small pieces because. . .

**Small questions and small solutions
lead to big change over time.**
Productivity is about sustainable improvement.
In order to achieve that you have to. . .

Look inward to reveal a way forward.
Dedicate specific times for reflecting on the
contents of your notebook. Prioritize what
matters, discard what doesn't.

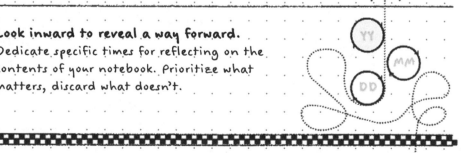

Failure is guaranteed if you never begin.
If you try and fail, you fail once. If you compromise
and fail, you fail twice as hard because you
know you didn't try. All you have to do is. . .

START!

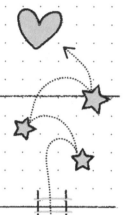

125

Better > Perfect

"The obstacle is the way."
—Ryan Holiday

??? !!!

The only thing you can control is the way you respond.
Focusing on things you can't control allows them to
control you. Focus on what you can control.

○ A
○ B
◉ C

To be useful, you must become useful, especially to yourself.
You can't improve the world around you if you can't improve
the world within. Choose your friends wisely, and be a friend
to yourself. To start this process. . . .

Study the good in your life.
Achievement is empty without
appreciation. If you can't appreciate
your hard work, what's the point?!
It's important to. . . .

GRATITUDE	GRATITUDE
- Promotion	
- Good dinner	
- Gift from Jamie	
- Thank you note	
- Created new job	
- Clean house	
11	12

Find the music in the mundane.
When you believe in what you're
doing, pain is transformed by purpose.

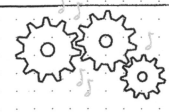

BEGINNING

*Many painters are afraid of the blank canvas, but the
blank canvas is afraid of the painter who dares and
who has broken the spell of "you can't" once and for all.*

—Vincent van Gogh

To dare in life is to make yourself vulnerable to the possibility of failure. Most of us don't welcome failure. So instead we avoid taking risks. We compromise, taking cold comfort in the assumption that we've removed the possibility of failure as we buckle up in the passenger seat and let life take the wheel.

The truth is, there's no avoiding failure. While failure may never feel good, failure in a life of compromise can be twice as devastating. Let's say you didn't take that exciting job overseas because it was easier to stay where you were. Then, out of nowhere, you lose your comfortable job. Now you have to contend with the loss of two jobs—one of which could have been a transformational experience. You'll never know, but chances are you'll never stop wondering what might have been.

Don't let fear dilute your life. Take, for example, Heather Caliri, who had struggled with performance anxiety since childhood. It hijacked her joy and her courage to try new things, take risks, and enjoy the things she loved most. There was no more obvious or bewildering example of this than her love of reading.

After having kids, she found less and less time to indulge her simple joy of sitting down with a book. She realized that performance anxiety had spread into her reading habits. She felt as if she didn't read enough, widely enough, or the right kinds of books. The more self-conscious she became about her reading habits, the harder it was for her to make time to read.

When she started Bullet Journaling, she was surprised at how motivating it was to "X" off boxes and how much she enjoyed the creativity of representing her daily life in beautiful ways in her notebook. Still, she hesitated to track her reading. *It'll only make me more anxious and aware that I'm not reading enough*, she thought. When she finally created a "Books Read" Collection, she was shocked to find that the opposite was true. She read a lot. The issue wasn't that she lacked motivation; it was that she walled herself off from trying, lest she fail.

Heather formed the habit of giving herself more credit for her efforts. The more she read, the more she felt at ease with herself. She began feeling the joy, excitement, and eagerness to read that she'd missed for years. Her Bullet Journal helped her to systematize her reading to overcome the barriers she'd felt. When we grant ourselves the opportunity to be rewarded by our courage, powerful things can happen.

There never has been, nor will there ever be, another like you. Your singular perspective may patch some small hole in the vast tattered fabric of humanity. Uniqueness alone, however, does not make you valuable. If you don't *do*, if you don't *dare*, then you rob the world—and yourself—of the chance to contribute something meaningful. As the French film director Robert Bresson once said, "Make visible what, without you, might perhaps never have been seen."[21] If you don't try something, it will assuredly never exist. Not your version, anyway. True, not all endeavors will be successful, but even our so-called failures can be valuable teachers.

We must take it upon ourselves to grow. We grow by learning, and we learn by daring to take action. There will always be risk, because we can't control the outcome. This is the way of life, and it's unavoidable. What is avoidable, however, is being perpetually haunted by all the things that could have been if you had only dared. Begin by giving yourself permission to believe you're worth the risk.

IN PRACTICE

Sometimes the hardest part of getting started is knowing where to begin. Maybe you just don't know how to start tackling your goals, your projects, your tasks, or even getting organized. Maybe you're afraid that you'll get it wrong or that you'll disappoint yourself. If that's the case, an easy place to begin is to get into the habit of simply capturing your thoughts on paper.

Start by taking notes on this book in your Bullet Journal. We will cover a lot of different ideas in Part III. I hope that some of the material will inspire new thoughts or provide information you find useful. Don't let it get away. Write it down.

Create a "Bullet Journal Method" Collection in your notebook. As you read, Rapid Log whatever comes to mind using the Bullets you learned about in Part II. Keep recording your thoughts as you make your way through the chapters, and you'll ease yourself into the system. Then figure out what you need next. Perhaps you'll add the Index, so you can find your Notes later on to refresh your memory.

Thoughts are the source of our goals, hopes, dreams, and ultimately our actions. An easy place to start with any endeavor is simply taking your thoughts out of your head and organizing them on paper. In so doing, you've already crossed the starting line to realize that it's just another moment. The only difference is that now you're behind the steering wheel.

REFLECTION

Know thyself.
—SOCRATES

William hat led you to open this book? What series of events led you here? Were you just browsing the shelf? Are you reading this because it was a gift and you don't want to hurt the gifter's feelings? (If that's the case, thank you for making it this far!) Or was there something missing you were hoping to find here? If so, how would you define that missing piece? How has it affected your life? Chances are these questions kicked up some dirt inside. It goes to show that no matter how simple an act may appear, it bears the legacy of countless bygone choices.

One of my favorite sculptures is called *The Thinker* by Auguste Rodin. It's the one with the naked guy sitting on a block, resting his head on his hand, you know, thinking. Like a lot of Rodin's work, it feels unfinished. Some surfaces appear rough; others lack detail. The visibility of these millions of minute choices imparts immediacy and humanity to his work—it's as though we can see the artist himself thinking.

Like a block of marble, our lives are finite. They start out rough and formless. Each choice we make places a chisel to the stone. Each action irreversibly chips away time. No action is so insignificant that it can't benefit from our attention. It's the lack of attention that's often responsible for the rubble of cringeworthy decisions weighing on our conscience.

To be sure, making bad decisions, no matter how smart or wise you are, is an unavoidable part of being human. Life is also an unruly medium. It slips, it shatters, it shifts, it crushes. Sometimes we even find ourselves on the receiving end of the chisel. It leaves us all rough around the edges. The beautiful thing is, as long as you're still alive, there is always material left to work with. Like *The Thinker*, your life doesn't have to be big, polished, or perfect to be beautiful. That said, we can do better.

Many poor decisions are born in the vacuum of self-awareness. We get so caught up in the doing of things that we forget to ask *why* we're doing them in the first place. Asking *why* is the first small but deliberate step we can take in the search for meaning.

The search for meaning often begins later than it needs to. Because it seems like such a monumental or esoteric undertaking, we tend to avoid this form of inquiry until it's forced on us by some shade of crisis or circumstance. Exploring our *why* from these dim places leaves us at a disadvantage. Our ability to see and think clearly is shrouded by our suffering. Soul-searching doesn't need to be confined to the dark seasons of our lives. It can be a gentle part of our everyday. It all begins with becoming mindful of how we're investing our time and energy—the things our Bullet Journal is faithfully recording for our reference.

You may be thinking, *Analyzing my to-do list isn't going to answer life's big questions.* Maybe, or maybe it's because we're untrained in the art of asking these types of questions. To understand the big intimidating *whys* (*What is the meaning of life? Why am I here?*), we start by asking the small *whys*: *Why am I working on this project? Why is my partner irritating me? Why am I feeling stressed?* In the Bullet Journal, we do this through the practice of Reflection.

Reflection is the nursery of intentionality. It grants us the protected mental environment we need to reclaim some much-needed perspective and begin to ask *why*. Through Reflection, we cultivate the habit of checking in with ourselves to examine our progress, our responsibilities, our circumstances, and our state of mind. It helps us see if we're solving the right problems, answering the right questions. It's by questioning our experience that we begin to sort the wheat from the chaff—the *why* from the *what*.

Don't worry, Reflection is not an invitation to flagellate yourself for past failures. It's an opportunity to harvest the rich information embedded in your lived experience and use it to fertilize your future.

Reflection helps identify what nourishes you so you can make better decisions as you seed the next season of your life.

Our lives are lived in seasons of more, seasons of less, seasons of triumph, seasons of loss. Each season sees our needs change. We live, learn, and adapt. So, too, must our definition of meaning.

Things that grow in one season rot in another. If we blindly hold on to the past, we'll be forced to sustain ourselves with the expiring beliefs from seasons gone by. No wonder we're often left feeling unsatisfied, empty, starving for substance.

In order to live fulfilling lives, we have to embrace the shifting nature of our experience by making our search for meaning an ongoing practice. This is why the Bullet Journal method has multiple Reflection mechanisms built right in. This is where the method shifts from a system into a practice by helping us continually chip away at what is unnecessary to reveal what is meaningful.

IN PRACTICE

Maybe you're thinking, *Ryder, I want to be a more reflective person, but I never have time. I need to be in the right headspace to think deep thoughts. My thoughts are all over the place, and so am I.*

If you're Bullet Journaling, then you've already begun. By keeping different types of logs, you're not only organizing your responsibilities, you're also documenting your thoughts and actions. It's a passive form of reflection! All you need to do now is transition at your own pace from passive reflection to active reflection.

Daily Reflection

Throughout the day, you're using your Daily Log (page 86) to simply capture your thoughts. Now it's just a matter of coming back to them. That's what Daily Reflection is designed for. It allows

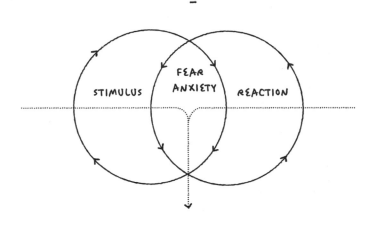

REACTIVITY

—

STIMULUS · FEAR ANXIETY · REACTION

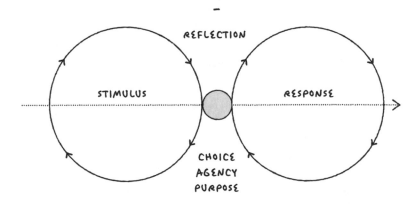

INTENTIONALITY

—

REFLECTION

STIMULUS · RESPONSE

CHOICE
AGENCY
PURPOSE

you to bookend each day with two dedicated times of active intro-spection.

AM Reflection: A Time to Plan

In the morning, or before you dive into your day, take a few moments to sit down with your Bullet Journal. If you're one of those people who wakes with a mind swelling with thoughts, now's the time to relieve that pressure. Offload anything that's bubbled up overnight. Clear your mind to make room for the day ahead. For those of you breakfast zombies, the AM Reflection helps get the gears turning.

Next, review all the pages of the current month to remind your-self of any open Tasks. This helps you focus and clarify your priori-ties and plan accordingly. You'll step into your day with confidence, clarity, and direction.

PM Reflection: A Time to Review

Where the AM Reflection favors planning to gear up for your day, the PM Reflection leans toward review to help you unwind. Before you go to bed, sit down with your Bullet Journal and scan what you've logged throughout the day. Mark completed Tasks with an "X." If a Task is missing, write it down. Again, you're unburdening your mind.

Once your journal is updated, bring your attention to each item individually. Here's where you begin to ask: *Why is this important? Why am I doing this? Why is this a priority?* And so on. This will help you surface distractions. Strike out the Tasks you've deemed to be irrelevant.

Finally, take a moment to appreciate your progress. Acknowledge the simple ways in which you've won the day. The PM Reflection can be a wonderful way to decompress before you sleep, relieving stress and anxiety through a sense of progress, preparedness, and purpose.

TIP: You can use your Daily Reflection as your daily digital detox window. After your PM Reflection, implement a "screens off" policy that lasts until you've completed your AM Reflection the following morning. It's a simple way to get yourself into the habit of unplugging.

Monthly and Yearly Reflection Through Migration

Technology is always moving us toward a more seamless existence. The less friction, the better. That's great when you're ordering pizza. You don't really need to understand all the miraculous tech that allows that hot cheesy goodness to appear out of thin air at your doorstep. Convenience, however, often comes at the expense of understanding. The less time you spend examining things, the less you know about them. When it comes to understanding how you spend your life, it's important to slow down and take the time.

Migration is designed to add the friction you need to slow down, step back, and consider the things you task yourself with. On the surface it's an automatic filtering mechanism, designed to leverage your limited patience. If something is not worth the few seconds it takes to rewrite it, then chances are it's really not important. In addition, handwriting triggers our critical thinking, helping us draw new connections between thoughts. As you migrate each item, you give yourself a chance to identify unconventional relationships or opportunities by holding each item under the microscope of your attention.

For everything we say yes to, we're saying no to something else. Migration gives you an opportunity to recommit to what matters and let go of what does not. As Bruce Lee once said, "It is not daily increase but daily decrease; hack away the unessential."

BULLET JOURNAL REFLECTION CYCLES

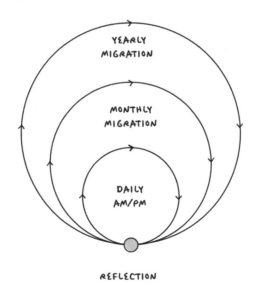

YEARLY MIGRATION

MONTHLY MIGRATION

DAILY AM/PM

REFLECTION

Consistency

I'm often asked how much time I spend on Daily Reflection. On average, I usually devote 5 to 15 minutes per session. It's not about how much time it takes; it's about being consistent. If you find yourself failing to check in for Reflection, reduce the amount of time you spend. Take as much or as little time as you need to make it part of your daily routine.

The goal is getting into the habit of checking in with yourself, asking small *whys*. Over time, you get better at answering these questions. You're refining your beliefs, your values, your ability to spot your weaknesses and your strengths. Slowly but surely you start to weed out distractions, which results in you steadily becoming more present and aware.

Awareness

In his beautiful commencement speech "This Is Water," at Kenyon College, author David Foster Wallace talked about the day-to-day and how "the so-called 'real world' will not discourage you from operating on your own default settings, because the so-called 'real world' of men and money and power hums along quite nicely on the fuel of fear and contempt and frustration and craving and the worship of self."[22]

He's talking about how, if we're not careful, we can start to go on autopilot, which can greatly diminish our experience of the world. During Reflection, we get in the habit of switching off our autopilot by examining our experience. This form of inquiry requires us to ask questions and not take things at face value. It encourages us to think about ourselves and the world in a more considered way.

Through consistently engaging with our experience, we become aware that even the dullest moment can have a hidden depth. As you cultivate your awareness, "it will actually be within your power to experience a crowded, hot, slow, consumer-hell-type situation as not only meaningful, but sacred, on fire with the same force that lit the stars—compassion, love, the subsurface unity of all things."[23]

Summary

When you go to the optometrist, you're asked to read symbols off a chart through a large metal device filled with lenses known as a phoropter. As you read, the optometrist switches lenses, asking you which brings the symbols into focus. Is it better now? Click. How about now? Click. The purpose is to find an array of lenses that alters the way light hits our retinas so that we may see with greater clarity.

When it comes to living a more intentional life, Reflection functions as a phoropter. It's the mechanism that helps improve our perception, but in order for it to work properly, we need to add the lenses. It's likely you already have some of your own, like your values and your beliefs. Reflection, however, is a rich and ancient practice. Each tradition offers its own lens through which we can correct our shortsightedness and sharpen our insight when we reflect. In the chapters that follow, I'll introduce you to the lenses I've found most useful. Let's explore these lenses designed to help us pull our life into greater focus.

MEANING

Eyes see only light, ears hear only sound, but
a listening heart perceives meaning.
—David Steindl-Rast

My favorite *Twilight Zone* episode is called "A Nice Place to Visit." It follows the story of a Mr. Valentine, a scrappy burglar gunned down by the police during a robbery, who is guided into the afterlife by an affable Englishman in a crisp white suit. To Valentine's surprise, he's ushered into luxury: an opulent New York penthouse, closets stocked with bespoke suits, bars brimming with the finest liquor. He showboats around town in fancy cars and wins game after game at the casinos surrounded by smitten socialites. Money, power, sex appeal—everything he ever wanted—finally his.

In time, though, the novelty fades. His joy withers to boredom. This perfect, longed-for existence reveals itself to be entirely unfulfilling. Valentine turns to his guide and says, "I don't think heaven is for me. I think I belong in the other place." Whereupon his guide wryly responds, "What makes you think this is heaven?"

Success often feels surprisingly empty. That holds true not just for financial success, but for the kind of self-improvement we've always thought to be healthy and good. In the article "How I'm Overcoming My Obsession with Constant Self-Improvement," Leo Babauta, the creator of the blog *Zen Habits*, writes about how he ran an ultramarathon, participated in the Goruck Challenge (a ten-hour obstacle course where you must wear a brick-filled backpack), and learned how to code, only to find that his life wasn't any better. "The fantasy was never real," he writes.[24] He is not alone in this realization.

The world is more literate, well-fed, vaccinated, and technologically advanced than ever. A hunger for more, however, is prompting millennials to spend nearly twice as much per month on self-improvement as Boomers (despite earning about half as much as the elder generation).[25] Which raises another question: How do we reconcile this trend with the escalating rates of depression? American youths suffering from severe depression increased from 5.9 percent in 2012 to 8.2 percent in 2015.[26] In the United States alone, anxiety disorders affect 40 million adults—that's 18.1 percent of the population.[27]

You might be thinking that getting fit and taking night classes are totally worthwhile goals. Maybe, but the impact of what you're doing is contingent on *why* you're doing it. The key is understanding the motivation underlying your hard work.

Our efforts are always fueled by some promise. What exactly do you expect in exchange for your blood, sweat, and tears? What is the goal behind all of our goals? For most of us, it's to be happy, and therein lies the problem.

Think back to the last goal you achieved. You pushed yourself hard, drawn by the potential and promise of a happier life. But when you finally crossed the finish line, what did you find? Did that raise, that new house, that car, that vacation, make you feel the way you hoped it would? Chances are the answer is no—or not for long, anyway. Why is that?

We can begin to untangle this conundrum by accepting a simple truth: None of us can know with any true certainty what will make us happy. In fact, it turns out that we're pretty lousy at guessing how something will make us feel, thanks to a phenomenon known as impact bias: "the tendency for people to overestimate the length or the intensity of future feeling states."[28] In essence, we chronically underestimate our ability to adapt.

As we race toward our goals, we learn new things, and our circumstances change. By the time we arrive at the finish line, we're simply different people. The best we can do is guess what will make us happy. So we place blind bets, gambling away our money, our time, and our sanity in the pursuit of happiness. It seems the harder we try to be happy, the more elusive happiness becomes. As comedian Tim Minchin once quipped, "Happiness is like an orgasm: If you think about it too much, it will go away."[29]

Speaking of which, our built-in drive for pleasure is another critical factor in understanding the enigmatic nature of happiness. We're built to adapt to heat, to cold, to hardship, and this is partially a result of our ability to experience pleasure. Pleasure allowed us to quickly discern good from bad, harmful from helpful. We like things that feel good, and we'll go out of our way for more of the good stuff, like shelter, sustenance, water.

In the bad old days, when we spent most of our time, you know, trying not to die, pleasure was limited and practical. Nowadays it's a commodity, marketed as a substitute for happiness, and it's on demand.

Thanks to our ability to rapidly adapt, even the most pleasurable experience or purchase quickly becomes the boring new normal. Soon we're itching for another quick fix of pleasure. No longer satisfied with what we already have, we treat our withdrawal pains by incrementally upping the dosage. More shoes, more booze, more sex, more food, more "likes," just *more*. This phenomenon is known as hedonic adaptation.

Exploiting what Sean Parker, founding member of Facebook, called this "vulnerability in human psychology" is the bread and butter of our economy.[30] Notice how much advertising focuses not on "good" but on "more": better, faster, fresher, stronger, lighter. "Good" is enough, but "better" is a promise of "happiness" that's just another transaction away.

What can be bought can be owned. That is the social contract. You buy shoes at the shoe store, clothes at the clothing store, cars at the dealership, and so on. Notice that there is no happiness store. It's not because it can't be bought; it's because happiness can't be owned.

Happiness, like sadness, comes and goes. It's an emotion, and like all emotions, it's blessedly temporary. Imagine a world in which our emotions calcified, forcing us to entertain our demons indefinitely. Or Valentine's heaven/hell, where things are so perfect, so lacking in contrast, that everything ultimately feels meaningless. It would poison us. In fact, we often define the inability to transition between emotional states as mental illness. Seen in this light, seeking some mythical state of perpetual happiness not only collides with reality, but seems undesirable.

So are all our goals, all our striving, ultimately pointless? Not in the least. It means that happiness itself can't be the goal. Clearly happiness is important, so the question becomes: How do we lure it into our lives?

When you look up the term, you'll find more than a dozen synonyms, demonstrating how complex and nuanced the experience can be, but none volunteers a way for us to be happy. This is the domain of philosophy, which, despite its stuffy reputation, was conceived to help us live better lives. One such philosophy is Greek eudaimonism, "a moral philosophy that defines right action as that which leads to the 'well-being' of the individual."[31] This idea of contented well-being as simply a by-product of personal industry is a recurring theme in a variety of philosophical traditions around the world. In other words, happiness is the result of our actions directed toward other goals.

> *If happiness is the result of our actions, then we need to stop asking ourselves how to be happy. Rather, we should be asking ourselves how to be.*

The people of Okinawa, Japan, for example, are among the happiest and longest-lived populations, with the world's highest ratios of centenarians at approximately 50 per 100,000.[32] When asked what their secret to happiness was, a common answer was *ikigai*. "Your *ikigai* is at the intersection of what you are good at and what you love doing," says author Héctor García. He writes, "Just as humans have lusted after objects and money since the dawn of time, other humans have felt dissatisfaction at the relentless pursuit of money and fame and have instead focused on something bigger than their own material wealth. This has over the years been described using many different words and practices, but always hearkening back to the central core of meaningfulness in life."[33]

Maybe we have it all backward. It seems that in our pursuit of happiness, we're taking our focus off of what could be meaningful. But it's in the pursuit of what is meaningful that happiness seems most likely to appear. As Viktor Frankl put it, "Happiness cannot be pursued, it can only ensue."[34]

The question becomes: What is meaningful? Many of us aren't sure, and that's okay. It's a profoundly complicated question that's been giving us headaches as long as we've had the heads to think about it. Academic definitions are vague by necessity to encompass the many subjective views of what's meaningful. We have experienced firsthand how our subjective definition of what is meaningful changes over time. Do you still treasure the same things as your twelve-year-old self? Probably not. What is clear is that there is no single meaning to life; there are many.

From service to faith to family to contribution, people are happy to volunteer all sorts of avenues toward meaning. Yes, they're all worthy, but it doesn't necessarily mean that *you* will find them fulfilling. I've met plenty of disillusioned volunteers, social workers, teachers, doctors, and even parents. They know that what they're doing is objectively meaningful, yet they just don't *feel* it.

What does feeling have to do with meaning? Arguably everything. There is no intellectualizing what resonates with you, and that's why it's so hard to define. When it reveals itself, you *feel* it. The Greeks had a term for this—*phainesthai*—which has been roughly translated at different times to "showing itself," "that which reveals itself," "shining forth," and "to appear."[35]

Your senses will witness what "shines forth," that which holds the promise of meaning.

If we live passive lives, ones where we don't pursue what shines forth, we remain in the dark, largely ignorant as to our place in the world. In this state, our efforts, no matter how well intentioned or noble, will often feel meaningless because they seem to serve no purpose. We try and fail to fill that void with things, which does little more than weigh us down even further. That's why it's vital to seek out what shines forth for you.

How do we uncover what "shines forth"? Just as we all have a built-in mechanism for seeing, we also have a built-in mechanism for sensing the luminous things that call to us: our curiosity.

Our curiosity is the exciting electricity we feel in the presence of potential. It sparks our imagination and wonder, drawing us out of ourselves and into the world. It's a magnetism that often supersedes reason, greed, personal gain, and even happiness. You've already experienced this in some form, be it attraction to a person, fascination with a topic, or the thrill of working on something you enjoy. Your curiosity can also be drawn toward things that you haven't experienced yet. Maybe it's the idea of raising a family, starting a company, making an album, or addressing a particular problem in the world. Whatever they may be, these are the things your heart has identified as potentially meaningful. The question is: Have you ever granted yourself a moment to define what exactly these things are?

Let's zoom way out. Before you join that gym, enroll in those classes, buy that TV, or even set goals, it helps to have some basic big-picture awareness that guides your actions. You need to take the time to articulate your vision for what it means to live a meaningful life based on your felt experience. If you don't orient yourself this way, you can lose yourself in "the other place," far removed from the things you care about. So let's start by figuring out what kind of life *you* want to lead, beginning with the following exercises.

IN PRACTICE

A TALE OF TWO LIVES

This thought experiment was inspired by the poem "The Road Not Taken" by Robert Frost. Imagine you are a traveler who arrives at a fork in the road. On one side is the well-worn path. On the other you find the path less traveled.

THE WELL-WORN PATH

This path leads you toward the familiar. It favors comfort over risk. It is a continuation of your current life. You simply move along in whatever pursuits are comfortable for you, putting little effort into changing your lesser qualities or striving for improvement. At the end of this life, what will you have accomplished, personally and professionally? What are the consequences of this life?

THE PATH LESS TRAVELED

This path leads you into the unfamiliar. It's a life that favors risk over comfort. You dare to pursue the things that interest you and actively work to improve yourself. At the end of this life, what will you have accomplished, personally and professionally? What are the consequences of this life?

Now (bear with me), **for each path**, take 15 minutes or more to write your obituary based on having taken that path. Create a "Two Lives" Collection and add it to your Index. Start with one spread for one path. Set up the second spread only when you've completed the first. Fill as many pages as you need. Dig deep. Be honest. This is for your eyes only. What do you see as you look far down each path?

Postmortem

1. Read through both obituaries. On the next page in your notebook, write yourself a letter. What realizations, emotions, questions, positives, or negatives came up during the exercise? What surprised you? What saddened or scared you? What excited you? The point is to capture how you feel about seeing your whole life flash before your eyes. Phrase it in a way to remind your future self—the one who will be reading this later—what shifted, because something definitely will. Remind yourself what you're trying to get away from, and where you want to go.

2. Select the life you liked best, and identify and circle the accomplishments that you're most proud of. Once you're done, migrate (page 107) these items into a "Goals" Collection (page 152). Just like that, you've taken your first step toward realizing a more meaningful life on your own terms. Let's keep going!

GOALS

We can do no great things;
only small things with great love.
—Mother Teresa

Curiosity points the needle of our inner compass toward the hopeful magnetism of possibility and meaning. It's the force that compels us to venture out of our comfort zone into unfamiliar territory filled with uncertainty and risks. The question becomes: How do we best harness our curiosity while reducing the risk of failure? We set goals. When set with intention, goals can provide structure, direction, focus, and purpose.

Goals give us the opportunity to
define what we want.

When not set with intention, goals can be knee-jerk reactions to something ugly or painful in our lives. If you're feeling overweight, for example, dedicating yourself to running a marathon that's a few months away is a reactionary goal—and likely a counterproductive one. Your chances of achieving that goal are slim, but the chances of hurting or disappointing yourself are high. When setting reactionary goals, you're likely to find yourself right back where you started: high risk, low reward.

Appropriating other peoples' goals is another common pitfall. "Make a million dollars," for example, is the kind of goal we hear bandied about, but it's not a meaningful one. Why? Because it serves no purpose; it's empty calories. Your goals need real substance in order to be sustainable. You need to understand exactly *why* you need a million dollars.

Your goals should be inspired by *your* felt experience. Surely you have sources of real passion in your life—whether the positive impetus of what brings you joy or painful lessons from the school of hard knocks. Put them to work! Both are powerful wells from which you can draw meaningful goals.

With that in mind, let's try again to set that big-money goal: "I want to make enough money to pay off my student loans, buy a two-bedroom house for my parents to retire in, and cover my kids' education."

This goal, by contrast—though still ambitious—has meaningful parameters. You know exactly how it would impact your life for the better. This is critical, because big goals take time and sustained effort to complete. Of all the challenges you'll face along the way, endurance often proves to be the most cunning and lethal adversary. Big goals therefore must be fueled by an authentic need that will help you weather the days, months, or even years it takes to fulfill them. That need must be strong enough to fortify you against the siren songs of distraction, excuses, and doubt that will beckon you toward the rocks. Angela Lee Duckworth, PhD, author of *Grit,* found that "perseverance and passion for long-term goals" indicated success "better than any other predictor."[36]

For some of us, perseverance and passion conjure images of no-pain-no-gain athletes scoring game-winning points or sticking landings on fractured limbs, eccentric creatives sacrificing all for art as they shiver in icy garrets, or monks spending decades meditating in silence. But passion and perseverance, like all emotional qualities, live on a spectrum. In an "all-or-nothing" world, we tend to forget the power of *something*. The mightiest tree sprouts from a vulnerable seed. The seed of passion is curiosity. The seed of perseverance is patience. By designing your goals strategically, you can begin to cultivate your opportunities by seeding both your patience and curiosity.

IN PRACTICE

CREATE A GOALS COLLECTION

Our ambitions often suffer from being little more than vague notions or abstract daydreams swimming around in our heads: "One day, I'll . . ." Let's start by capturing our ideas on paper so we can transform them into actionable goals.

If you haven't done so already, create a Goals Collection in your Bullet Journal on the next blank spread. Big or small, just write them down here so you have them clearly contained in one reusable place. In doing so you've already taken the first important step to realizing them.

This Collection serves as a menu of sorts, listing your potential futures. It can keep you focused and motivated, but even the greatest menu is useless if you don't order. The next step is to start nudging yourself toward action. Otherwise it's easy to hoard goals, waiting for just the right moment to get started. That moment will never come. We have to create our own opportunities, because life doesn't wait.

THE 5, 4, 3, 2, 1 EXERCISE

A great way to get motivated is by realizing just how limited your time really is. The *5, 4, 3, 2, 1* exercise is designed to help you contextualize your goals in terms of time. It will quantify your objectives by breaking them down over the short, mid, and long term. If you're struggling to tackle your goals, give this a try.

First, turn to your next blank spread. The Topic for this new Collection will be "5, 4, 3, 2, 1." Divide the spread into five rows on each page (page 154). The left page will be for your personal goals; the right page will be for your professional goals. The top cell will store the goals you want to accomplish in 5 *years*. In the next cell you'll have goals you want to achieve in 4 *months*; the next cell will be for goals to achieve in 3 *weeks*; the next cell will be for goals to attain in 2 *days*; and the final cell will be for goals you intend to accomplish in the next 1 *hour*.

Now turn back to your "Goals" Collection and migrate your goals into their appropriate cells. It does not have to line up exactly, but the idea is to start the process by defining the amount of time and energy (perseverance and passion) your goals require, both individually and as a whole. It will provide some much needed context.

5, 4, 3, 2, 1 —PERSONAL

5 YEARS

- Start a family
- Own a property
* - Fluency in another language

LONG-TERM GOALS

4 MONTHS

* - Travel to Hawaii
- Lose 10 pounds
- Visit Niclas

3 WEEKS

- Donate clothes
- Volunteer

MID-TERM GOALS

2 DAYS

- Clean out closet
- Clean kitchen
* - Get driver's license renewed

1 HOUR

- Clean fridge
* - Call parents
- Make reservation for Leah dinner

SHORT-TERM GOALS

PRIORITIZE YOUR GOALS

Once you've plotted out your goals, consider them individually. Are they worth the amount of time you think they will take? If not, cross them off. Prioritize the remaining items. Which ones really resonate with your experience? Which ones shine forth brighter than the others? Mark them with the priority Signifier "*".

If you're implementing the 5, 4, 3, 2, 1 exercise, you may only prioritize one goal in each cell (page 155). Personal and professional pages should be graded separately, leaving you with ten priorities total.

Add your four short-term goals (those in the hour and day cells) to your Daily Log and set them as priorities with a "*" Signifier. Knock them out first to build the momentum you need to tackle your bigger goals. That takes care of four of your ten goals! The remaining goals all get their own separate Collection; for example, "Travel to Hawaii" or "Gain fluency in another language."

If you hesitate to create six new Collections (three personal, three professional), perhaps it's an indicator that some of your goals aren't as important as you thought. That's okay, strike them out. It's not about how many goals you have. It's about working on what matters.

FOCUS ON YOUR PRIORITIES

Once your Collections are set up, take a moment to promise yourself not to revisit your "Goals" or "5, 4, 3, 2, 1" Collections until the ones you picked are either complete or have become irrelevant. If you're an ambitious person, a list of potential projects can be very distracting. The thought of beginning something new can be alluring, especially if what you're currently working on is dragging out. Resist! Living intentionally is about focusing on what's most important now. Keep this in mind when picking your goals: What do you want to put into your life now—and, more importantly, *why*?

We want to be working on the fewest number of things possible. What?! Wouldn't it be more effective to be multitasking? No, we want to keep multitasking to an absolute minimum. Why? Studies suggest that only around 2 percent of the population is psychologically able to multitask.[37] The rest of us aren't multitasking; we're simply juggling. We're not working on things simultaneously; we're actually micro-tasking: rapidly switching between tasks—struggling not to drop the balls.

When you leave a Task unfinished and move quickly onto something else, you leave part of your attention behind you, stuck to that project you were just working on. University of Minnesota professor Sophie Leroy, PhD, calls this "attention residue." She writes that "people need to stop thinking about one task in order to fully transition their attention and perform well on another. Yet, results indicate it is difficult for people to transition their attention away from an unfinished task and their subsequent task performance suffers."[38] In other words, the more thinly you slice your attention and time, the less focused you become. The less focused you become, the less progress you make. This is why you may feel like you're not getting a lot done even though you're "super busy."

Attend to your core priorities. Use them as a barrier to prevent other distractions from leaking in. Go through them systematically, focusing as much attention as possible on one thing at a time. Give your goals the opportunity they deserve to reveal their lessons by focusing on the process. It's arguably the process, rather than the goals themselves, that will prove to be most valuable. The process accounts for the majority of the experience and therefore provides the bulk of the information that will help you grow.

BREAK DOWN YOUR GOALS INTO SPRINTS

When I was very young, all I wanted to do in life was to be a stop-motion animator. I grew up endlessly rewatching movies inspired by the Arabian Nights and Greek myths, featuring fantastic creatures designed by Ray Harryhausen. That, I told myself, was what I wanted to do, no question, no doubt . . . until I did it.

I eventually shot a short stop-motion piece with a friend. It turned out reasonably well for a movie with the whopping budget of frozen pizza and some clay. I learned a lot working on that project, but most importantly I learned that pursuing this career would leave me one fry short of a Happy Meal. Sure, the realization was a bit heartbreaking, but it was also a relief. It freed me to explore other things. Now I never look back and wonder what might have been.

Not all things we're into are meant to be our occupation. That in itself is a valuable lesson to learn, especially when you're young. It's important to figure out what role the things that interest you play in your life. Not every hobby or curiosity is a calling, but some are. We figure that out by safely trying them on for size for a short period of time before making a major commitment. Note that I tried out stop-motion animation in a small way, on a short-term project, before committing myself to a major goal like applying to an animation program at a film school.

Breaking down long-term goals into smaller, self-contained goals can turn what seems like a marathon into a series of Sprints. Sprints cover the same ground, just in shorter, more manageable intervals. This technique is a slightly adapted variation of a similar approach deployed in agile software development, but it can be powerful for tackling any type of goal.[39] Even more modest-size goals can usually be broken down into smaller goals that can fit into the most impatient person's life (I fit that description).

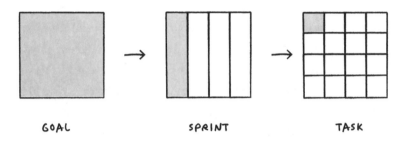

GOAL SPRINT TASK

Breaking down goals into Sprints mitigates the risks of being overwhelmed and fatigued. If you're no good in the kitchen but you're determined to change that, don't start by serving soufflés to six of your fancy foodie friends. Even if it all works out, the pressure may make the experience so unpleasant that you'll risk spoiling your curiosity for cooking altogether. Feelings of hardship can quickly eclipse those of curiosity or satisfaction. Start with a smaller, simpler dish, and see how you feel when it's done.

How are Sprints different from just dividing a goal into phases? Unlike phases, which are not ends in themselves, Sprints are independent, self-contained projects—thus the outcome is, let's hope, a source of satisfaction, information, and motivation to keep going (or, as happened with my stop-motion animation project, a helpful cue to let this particular goal go).

One author and entrepreneur, for example, was curious about podcasting. It was something he knew little about. Rather than dedicating himself to becoming a podcaster, he set out to do six episodes with his friend Kevin Rose. That experiment turned into *The Tim Ferriss Show*, the number one business podcast on iTunes, with over 200 episodes and over 100 million downloads. It goes to show that we shouldn't underestimate the potential impact of small, focused projects. The first version of bulletjournal.com was also the result of a Sprint.

To set up Sprints, structure them around specific subset goals or skills needed for a longer-term goal. To return to the cooking analogy, here's how that might look:

LONG-TERM GOAL: LEARN HOW TO COOK

Possible Sprints:

- Learn knife skills
- Learn how to sear and sauté [adding Tasks for other methods as you go]
- Learn how to select fresh vegetables [leveling up to Tasks for selecting fruits, meats, poultry, etc.]
- Learn how to cook eggs [setting up related Tasks one by one: hard-boiled, scrambled, over easy, an omelet]

SPRINT REQUIREMENTS:

1. **Have no major barriers to entry** (nothing preventing you from starting). For example, to learn knife skills, you don't have to purchase an entire expensive set of chef's knives. You just need a basic kitchen utility knife that you may already own or can buy with minimal investment.

2. **Consist of very clearly defined, actionable Tasks.** Your knife skills might be broken down into holding a knife properly, sharpening, peeling, slicing, dicing, cubing, mincing, and so on.

3. **Have a fixed, relatively short time frame for completion** (should take less than a month to complete, ideally a week or two). Just making a salad several days a week and mastering a simple vegetable soup recipe would get your knife skills up to speed pretty quickly.

Following these three rules will keep your Sprints focused, actionable, and manageable. When structured correctly, it should be hard to come up with a valid excuse to postpone a Sprint. If you think a Sprint will take longer than a month, just split it into two smaller Sprints.

The point is to safely indulge your curiosity and try things on for size, without wasting time.

BRAIN STORM

Before we can break down our goal, we have to wrap our head around it. Now that you've picked your goal and created a Collection for it in your Bullet Journal, use the first spread to brainstorm the *what* and the *why*. Dig in and explore. Write down whatever comes to mind. This process gets your gears turning. Suppose your "Learn to Cook" goal brainstorming page looks like this:

1. What about this goal sparked my curiosity?

   I've always wondered how foods go from just sitting in the store to being a beautiful, nutritious meal on a plate. What happens, exactly?

2. What motivated me to want to invest my time and energy here?

   I'm spending a lot on take-out and prepared foods, and I know it's not the healthiest way to eat. I've gained a little weight lately and want to watch my calories.

3. What am I trying to accomplish?

   By learning to cook, I can save money and eat more healthfully, and I hope to lose a few pounds. I also want to be able to invite friends or a date over for a meal and not worry about screwing things up.

4. What will it require?

   Learning basic food-prep skills, basic cooking skills, and some easy go-to recipes for my own meals and a few crowd-pleasers like chili, soup, or burgers.

5. What is my definition of success with this goal?

   Spending less on take-out and prepared foods, healthier diet, and having friends over for dinner.

When you're done brainstorming, you should have a better idea of your goal's requirements: its scope, its milestones, and why it's important to you.

Now break it up into Sprints. Each Sprint can be laid out in another Subcollection (page 102) in your Bullet Journal. Next, you'll break each sprint down even further into Tasks.

Once you've listed out your Tasks, start figuring out how much time each Sprint would take. If you've ever had the privilege of working with a contractor, the same adage applies here: Take the time estimate and triple it. Progress is more important than speed. If something gets done more quickly than anticipated, great! There's nothing wrong with getting something done faster than expected (as long as you're not focusing on speed). What we want to avoid is falling behind. That tips our pleasure/pain scale toward the pain side and makes it harder for us to stick with the process. If you have the time, use it to your advantage. If you don't, reduce the scope of your Sprint.

Once you have your Sprints planned, block them out on the Calendar of your choice. Lock in a dedicated time to work through your Tasks. Now you know when the project begins, how long it will take, when to work on it, and when it ends.

The longer a goal takes to accomplish, the more it taxes your motivation. When motivation runs dry, goals tend to crumble. Sprint projects will help you reduce the load so you can enjoy the satisfaction of seeing regular progress. How you feel about a project is vital to its success, especially for personal endeavors, where you may not have a team or a boss to help you stay on task. Progress provides momentum. Momentum helps you cultivate your patience.

A writer living in Sweden, Olov Wimark believes one reason he

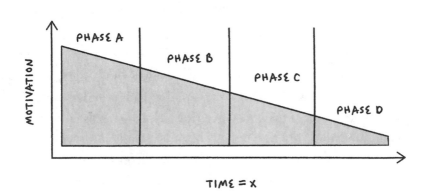

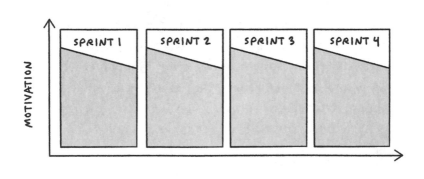

fell into depression is that it felt like his task list never got shorter. He was using an app that erased a task whenever he checked it off his list. His breakthrough came when his computer crashed and he started using an old typewriter. "I found that I wasn't all that hard on myself for a typo. Since I couldn't edit out what was already written, I had to live with what I wrote or rewrite the entire page. Words started to really flow out of me. And lo and behold, when evening came, there was a stack of work that had been done sitting in a pile next to the typewriter. I started feeling good about my accomplishments again." Similarly, he says, "the Bullet Journal is very tangible. Progress is apparent and reviews happen continuously, every time you open it to make a new notation." He filled an old reservoir pen with blue-gray ink and went to town. "Everything left open in my old system got transferred, planned, processed, or simply ignored."

Dividing larger goals into Sprints also acts as damage control. Perhaps one Sprint doesn't work out. You realize that it's not for you, or you come across information or a situation that throws a wrench into the gears. If you planned your Sprint well, shutting it down won't derail you from related Sprints. At worst, you may have to shuffle around your schedule a bit.

Successful or not, Sprints provide you with room for reflection. In addition to Daily Reflection (page 134)—which you can apply to your projects, not just your Daily Log—you have an opportunity after each Sprint to pause and reflect on the experience thus far. For example:

1. *What am I learning about my strengths, my weaknesses?*
2. *What's working, and what isn't?*

3. *What could I do a bit better next time?*
4. *What value was added to my life?*

Perhaps you discover that you need to refine your master goal, given what you learned along the way. That's great! Suppose you realize that you just want to cook Italian food, or that you only want to cook for large groups of people, or that you're much more interested in growing food than cooking it. Whatever the case may be, these realizations will help you dial in your goal, allowing you to allocate your time and energy more effectively. Course correction just means you've uncovered something even more meaningful, and that's the point. Just reapply the lessons you learned from the last Sprint to the next Sprint. This self-perpetuating cycle allows you to continually grow as you close in on what matters.

SMALL STEPS

I had three friends who shared three things in common: a soul-crushing desk job, a passion for yoga, and, at one point, a totally idyllic Instagram feed. You know the ones: posts of pristine white beaches bordered by lush palms and sky-blue waters. Endless images of beautiful people laughing their way through coconut cocktails, lounging around beach bonfires.

The first, let's call her Karen, quit her job, sold all her stuff, and moved to Costa Rica to become a yoga instructor. A year later she was right back at her desk. Why? She said that she didn't enjoy teaching yoga to entitled tourists at a resort. She had wanted to travel the world and experience local cultures. It didn't occur to her that locals couldn't afford to pay her to teach yoga and that working on the road greatly reduced the pleasure of travel. It was the same grind, just with better weather, but far away from the people she loved.

The second, let's call her Rachel, also quit her job for a yoga teaching position at a dreamy beach resort. A little over a year later, she resumed being a desk jockey. Her reason? She realized that teaching yoga took the fun out of it for her. What was once her treasured refuge became a job—and a much more physically strenuous one at that.

The last, let's call her Leigh, quit her office job a decade ago and has never looked back. She teaches yoga all around the world. What made her experience different? She started small. She began with teaching one class a week on weekends while still working her nine-to-five. An avid traveler, she used her vacations to experiment with teaching for a week or two at various resorts. It wasn't for her. Nothing lost, knowledge gained. Next, she tested being a guest instructor on retreats. Bingo. She loved retreats. They were intimate, fun, and profitable enough. The experience also gave her ideas for how she could improve on the retreat model. She started organizing her own local retreats. As they built steam, she moved them to more tropical places. And so it went. Rather than uproot her life, Leigh took a systematic approach to accomplishing her goal. She approached change with patience and curiosity, gradually figuring out one piece of the puzzle at a time. That inquisitive-yet-methodical approach ultimately allowed her to successfully transition into and sustain a very different kind of life.

Change is critical to productivity and growth—personal, professional, or otherwise. It can be a powerful way to alter our circumstances, but it can backfire. Large changes trigger our fear response. The more afraid we are, the more we need to calm ourselves. Many a great productive gesture or action has resulted in an equal or greater measure of inactivity. Peaks where we believe anything is possible are followed by shadowed valleys where we think maybe nothing is.

So how do we effect change in a way that is sustainable without stressing ourselves out? In Japan, there is a concept known as *kaizen*. *Kai* roughly translates to "change," and *zen* translates to "good"—thus, "good change." Another translation, perhaps tellingly, is "continual improvement."

Unlike in the West, where "disruption" is a buzzword for our favorite flavor of progress, *kaizen* focuses on surfacing opportunities for incremental improvement. It's an approach to problem-solving that takes the form of small questions like: *What little thing can we change to improve the situation? What could be done better the next time?* This is a powerful way to suss out achievable improvements, which makes it much easier to enjoy continued progress.

Though *kaizen* originated as a method to improve the quality and company culture of the Japanese automotive industry, its application is universal. When applied to our daily lives, *kaizen* can become a critical change agent. By bringing our attention to the little things, we can effect change while we avoid overwhelm. All we need to do is solve one small problem at a time. Each solution builds on those that came before it, and therefore these small steps add up quickly, effecting massive change over time.

IN PRACTICE

ASK SMALL QUESTIONS

In the Goals chapter (page 150), we discussed how to accomplish your goals by breaking them down into smaller self-contained Sprints. Now let's take these Sprints and break them down into actionable steps, or Tasks.

Create your Tasks through the lens of curiosity rather than by giving yourself commands or ultimatums. It's the difference between "Lose weight!" and "What one unhealthy thing could I remove from my diet?"

Our minds respond well to questions because we're problem

solvers. You can engage your curiosity by asking yourself questions to spark your imagination:

- *What do I want to do?*
- *Why do I want to do it?*
- *What small thing can I do right now to get started?*

Keeping your questions small helps the resulting Tasks remain manageable. The harder the Task, the more effort it will require and the more likely you'll be to put it off. Make the Tasks as effortless as possible.

You can also apply this technique if you come to a standstill in your project. Even if you're held up by something or someone, chances are there's still an action you can take to keep the project moving forward. Ask yourself questions such as:

- *What small step can I take now to move this forward?*
- *What could I improve now?*

It might be something as simple as researching relevant information on the internet, asking a few questions of a knowledgeable friend or colleague, recalibrating your Sprints, or writing a long-form entry in your notebook about what you've learned so far. Challenging yourself to find opportunities for incremental improvement will often yield a way forward. It's a simple way of training yourself to become more proactive.

The most powerful application of this technique is for problem-solving. The Bullet Journal method did not appear fully formed. It was slowly assembled by solving one challenge at a time. Over the years, most of the solutions I tested *didn't* work. Yet I wouldn't describe those efforts as failures. Each attempt that missed the mark taught me something new, which ultimately led to a better solution. In the words of Aleksandr Solzhenitsyn: "Mistakes are a great educator when one is honest enough to admit them and willing to learn from them."

When you run into issues, take a step back and start to tease them apart by asking small questions like:

- *What exactly did not work?*
- *Why did it not work?*
- *What small thing can I improve next time?*

Whatever obstacles or challenges you may encounter along the way, meet them with curiosity. Embrace them and examine them by asking small questions. Don't let fear, pride, or impatience deprive you of the opportunity to ask. As Carl Sagan once said, "There are naïve questions, tedious questions, ill-phrased questions, questions put after inadequate self-criticism. But every question is a cry to understand the world. There is no such thing as a dumb question."[40]

ITERATION

Once we have answers, we need to check them because they'll often be wrong. That's okay. It's simply part of the process of finding a solution. Thomas Edison supposedly once quipped, "I have not failed, I just found 10,000 ways that won't work." There's benefit and utility in failure. When actively embraced as a learning mechanism, it can help us grow. Rather than perceiving failure as an end, it should be redefined as an essential part of the creative process, the unavoidable precursor to success. For example, Sir James Dyson, inventor of the Dyson vacuum cleaner, tested 5,126 prototypes to produce the results he wanted. Now he's valued at over $4 billion.[41]

Edison, Dyson, and many others like them honor their failures by actively reapplying the lessons they learned. "Failure" allowed them to refine their ideas over and over again until they finally arrived at a solution that worked. This is known as the iterative cycle, which powers *kaizen.*

Iteration sounds more complicated than it is. Once you ask yourself a small question, like *What small thing can I change to make this better?*, you've already started a process known as the Deming Cycle, after W. Edwards Deming, the father of *kaizen.*[42] The Deming Cycle provides us with a four-stage framework for continual improvement: "Plan ⟶ Do ⟶ Check ⟶ Act." Let's break that down.

1. **Plan:** Recognize an opportunity and plan a change.
2. **Do:** Put the plan into play and test the change.
3. **Check:** Analyze the results of your test and identify what you've learned.
4. **Act:** Act on what you've learned. If the change didn't work, go through the cycle again with a different plan. If you were successful, incorporate what you learned to plan new improvements. Rinse and repeat.

Now, let's see how you can implement this in your Bullet Journal. Each day can be viewed as an iterative cycle. The most straightforward way is to *plan* during your AM Reflection (page

DAILY SCHEDULE

7

              AM Reflection

8

9

10

              Priorities

11

12

1   Lunch

2

3

4   Tasks

5

6

7   Dinner

8

9   Personal Priorities

10

11

              PM Reflection

12

Plan

Do

Check

Act

172

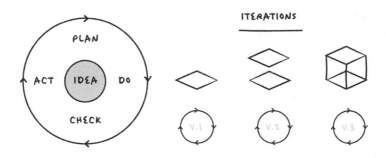

136), *do* during the day, and *check* and *act* during your PM Reflection.

As with all things Bullet Journal, this is not the only way it can be applied. You can run iterative cycles whenever you like—daily, weekly, even during your Monthly Migration (page 108). What's important is that it becomes a regular part of your approach.

Productivity is in large part a matter of consistency. Once you get it out of your head that you have to work at breakneck speed, you can focus on the process. Short of superhuman willpower, that's the only way you'll keep at it.

BETTER DAYS

This may all seem like a lot of work, especially if you're feeling low, stuck, or overwhelmed. You tell yourself that you lack the money, energy, time, or will to tackle your professional goals, let alone your personal ones. Just because these thoughts are real does not make them true. Even at the very bottom, you have a choice.

You can choose to focus on all the reasons why you can't, or you can look for some small way in which you *can*. If you're not happy with your life, then ask yourself, *What tiny thing could I do tomorrow that would make my life a little bit better?* Perhaps it's calling a friend, leaving a few minutes early to take the scenic route to work on a fine day, or tackling the chair that's drowning in your clothes. Again, we're looking for *any* win, no matter how small. Set the bar so low that you'll actually do it, and log it as a Task in your Bullet Journal.

Ask yourself the same question the next day. Find something, *anything*, that will make your life a little better. Perhaps catch up with another friend whose name came up during yesterday's call, try getting coffee from that funky little place you discovered on the scenic route, or sort one dresser drawer.

Continue doing this every day for a month, and keep track of it in your Bullet Journal. Before you know it, you'll have reconnected with people you care about, found fun new places, and enjoyed returning to a home that is less of a disaster. You've narrowed that gap between where you are and where you want to be. This is how small actions inspired by small questions can have an exponential positive impact on your life. Question by question, task by task, you're cultivating a sustainable path toward continual improvement and good change, one small step at a time.

28 THINGS BETTER

	22	23	24	25	26	27	28	WEEK 4
15	16	17	18	19	20	21		WEEK 3
8	9	10	11	12	13	14		WEEK 2
1	2	3	4	5	6	7		WEEK 1

TIME

In the end it's not the years in your life
that count, it's life in your years.
—Abraham Lincoln

When asked to describe his theory of relativity, Einstein (mercifully) paraphrased it like this: "When a man sits with a pretty girl for an hour, it seems like a minute. But let him sit on a hot stove for a minute and it's longer than any hour. That's relativity."[43] In other words, our perception of time changes relative to what we are doing.

Just think about how different our perception of time is now compared to when we were kids. Back then, an hour-long car ride seemed to last forever. Are we there yet? The older we get, the less sensitive we become to the passage of time and the less mindful we are about how we spend it. Deadline after deadline, goal after goal, time races by, especially when we're busy. Because our experience of time is so relative, it's easy to forget that it's a finite resource. Before we know it, we're out of time.

*The hard truth is that we can't "**make time**," we can only "**take time**."*

Though we can't make more, we *can* increase the quality of the time we take.

Measuring the quality of time is not an exact science, but a key indicator is impact. How often have you sat at your desk all day, yet felt like you accomplished very little? Conversely, sometimes you sit down for a few hours and crank out a few days' worth of work. It has little to do with the amount of time you had; it's about how much attention you were able to bring into the present moment. Reining in your attention can prove difficult because our minds are incompetent time travelers. They have a tendency to get lost in both the past and the future. How often do we catch ourselves fixating on things we can't change, or worrying about things we can't predict? That's a lot of time and energy siphoned away from the only place where we can actually make a difference: the here and now.

The quality of our time is determined by our ability to be present.

Our attention lives on a spectrum. On one side are things that repel our curiosity, like going to the DMV. On the opposite side of the spectrum is a state often referred to as "flow," where we are most present and can have the most impact.

Mihaly Csikszentmihalyi, PhD, the Hungarian psychologist who coined the term, spent his career studying what makes people happy. During his research he interviewed creatives from all fields, from painters to poets to scientists. All described an ideal state in which their work seemed to take on a life of its own. Some described it as ecstatic. The root of the word "ecstasy" comes from the Greek *ekstasis*, which means "standing outside oneself." Csikszentmihalyi posits that this feeling is the result of the mind being so consumed with a task that it cannot consciously process the experience of self.[44] We enter flow when we're fully engaged. It's here, when we're totally present, that we unlock our full productive and creative potential. So is it possible to create flow? Flow, like happiness, is something that can't be forced. By being strategic with our use of time, however, we can create the conditions where flow is more likely to occur.

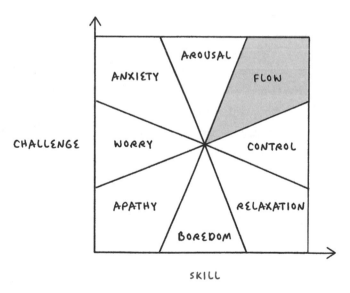

Based on the work of Mihaly Csikszentmihalyi, PhD

IN PRACTICE

TIME BOXING

No matter how intentional your life may be, you probably have some responsibilities that are not necessarily enjoyable, but are unavoidable. We all do. Some may seem difficult, which scares us (having that heart-to-heart with our significant other, approaching our boss about a raise, giving a big presentation). Others may seem too easy, which bores us (cleaning the house, paying bills, routine stuff at work). We tend to put off both types of activities as long as we can. Of course they don't just disappear; they tick away on our Task list like time bombs. The longer we put them off, the more of a priority they become. That's how piddly stuff like paying bills becomes an energy-zapping, time-sucking, undeserving emergency of late charges, low balances, and financial angst that blows up in your face.

We can defuse these obligations through time boxing. As its name suggests, time boxing quarantines an activity to an allotted slot of time. It's designed to bring your full attention to something by only allowing you to focus on it for a predefined period of time.

Time boxing adds two key motivational ingredients to a Task you've been putting off: structure and urgency.

If you only have 30 minutes a day to read something you will be tested on, you'll make those 30 minutes count. You're making it painless enough to temper your impatience ("This won't drag on, thank goodness"), simple enough that you won't get overwhelmed ("This I can do!"), and challenging enough to engage your attention ("Okay, 30 minutes to get my head into this. Brain, we've got this. Go!").

Let's say you have to file your taxes in a month. Rather than waiting until the last minute and realizing that there's all sorts of stuff that you didn't take into account and then stressing out about it, break it down into time-boxing sessions. For example:

— Sessions 1–2: Sun., 8:30–9:00 p.m.—Gather materials.
— Sessions 3–6: Mon., Wed., Sun., 8:30–9:00 p.m.—Compile materials into spreadsheet.
— Session 7: Tues., 8:30–9:00 p.m.—Wrap up and submit files.
— Session 8: Thurs. (last day), 8:30–9:00 p.m.—Provide any additional info.

The key to creating flow is balancing the challenge of a task with your skill level. If you lack the skills for a given Task, then that Task can quickly cause anxiety and feel overwhelming. Time boxing allows you to whittle away at a Task and incrementally improve your skill in the process. Over time, this can reduce how challenging something is. If on the other hand a task requires little to no effort, then our ability to engage is also very low. In this context, time boxing can be used to increase the challenge by creating a sense of urgency.

SCHEDULING: DON'T PUT IT OFF, PUT IT FIRST

Our attention span drains throughout the day. *When* we do something has a large impact on how well we do it. If there's something you find yourself putting off, then you've identified your chore. Procrastination indicates that it may be the most challenging Task on your list, because it worries you or doesn't interest you. Put it first.

I fully appreciate not wanting to start the day with something that's not exciting or motivating. All the more reason to just get it out of the way. It's the pebble in your shoe. Take it out before it makes real trouble. Front-loading your day with the easy stuff is its own form of procrastination. Getting more onerous chores out of the way first makes the rest of the day feel easier. Like when running with weights on, you feel lighter and stronger as soon as they come off.

Another benefit to this reverse hierarchy of Tasks is that you're working your way toward the things that interest you the most. It's much easier to maintain focus and motivation throughout the day when you have something to look forward to. That being said, we all have different biorhythms. Some people light up at night. The trick is to figure out when you're most focused and productive, and plan accordingly.

MEMENTO MORI

It had been a year since I had last talked to my grandfather. I knew his health was failing, so I wrote "Call Grandy" in my Bullet Journal. But before I got around to it, he was gone. Most everyone I know has a similar story, a similar regret. Death provides the most salient reminder of the value of time.

The Romans had a phrase, *memento mori*, which roughly translates to "remember death." Legend has it that when the generals returned victorious from battle and paraded down the street, they had a servant whisper this phrase into their ear over and over, to keep them humble and focused.

That all living things must die is one of the few absolute truths we will ever know. Yet, in the West, we all but demonize impermanence. Death is anthropomorphized as the Grim Reaper, a ghoulish enemy looming in the shadows, waiting to take everything from us. It's a terrifying notion that makes our relationship with the inevitable very one-sided. It doesn't need to be this way. Embracing the reality of impermanence can make the time we have significantly richer.

Think of your favorite food. Let's say it's pizza. Suppose that one day you're told that you will get to enjoy pizza eighty-seven more times in your life. Does this make you dislike, avoid, and dread eating pizza? Does pizza become depressing? No, it would likely be the opposite. Simply being aware that it's limited heightens your ability to experience it, to be more present, to savor each bite with an appreciation that had been unavailable to you before.

Steadily reminding yourself that you, your insufferable colleague, your pet, your lover, your sibling, your parent will die can fundamentally improve the nature of your interactions with all. It can make you more empathetic, forgiving, patient, kind, and grateful. Most of all, it can improve the quality of your time by helping you to become more present.

Marcus Aurelius, emperor of Rome and Stoic philosopher, once said: "You could leave life right now. Let that determine what you do, say, and think."[45] How would your life change if you truly operated under those directives? Would everything stay the same? What would you *do* differently? What would you *say* differently? Did simply *thinking* this way pull things into greater clarity or offer a new perspective? The real question is: Why don't we already operate this way? After all, this is the reality we inhabit.

We can't always control what fate drops in our lap. In the moments where we do have a choice, we must be vigilant about what we let into our days because we don't have life to spare. During Migration we ask ourselves "what is vital" and "what matters" to help us filter out distractions from our lives. Sometimes they're hard questions to answer. Adding this lens of impermanence to your Reflection can provide clarity by reminding you of what's at stake. We remember death so we don't forget to make the most out of our time alive.

GRATITUDE

Life is so subtle that sometimes you barely notice yourself
walking through the doors you once prayed would open.

—BRIANNA WIEST

There's a scene in David Lynch's *Twin Peaks* where Special
Agent Dale Cooper and Officer Harry S. Truman walk into
the quaint Double R diner. As they enter, Agent Cooper taps Officer Truman on the chest, smiling, and says, "I'm going to let you in
on a little secret. Every day, once a day, give yourself a present."

The present? An order of two cups of "good, hot, black coffee."

There is something deeply touching about this scene. In the
weird, violent, and questionable sanity of the Lynchian world sur-
rounding him, Cooper found a way to inject his life with some
lightness.

He's taking stock of the good. He loves this diner, he loves this
coffee, and he's granting himself a moment to take it all in and appreciate it. Though he claims that this ritual is a secret, I would
argue that it's an underrated skill available to us all.

In the meditative tradition of mindfulness, we're taught to bring our attention into the moment. Be it doing the dishes, brushing our teeth, or standing in the checkout line, we're fully there, cultivating our ability to be present. A common misconception about meditation is that it's about getting rid of thoughts. Rather, mindfulness helps distance yourself from them. A helpful metaphor shared by one of my teachers was that if thoughts were cars, meditation helps us stand on the side of the road rather than getting stuck in traffic.

It's easy to get so caught up in the traffic of our lives that we can easily pass right by even the most important of moments. A glowing example of this is how we fixate on achievement. If achievement is a defining measure of productivity, then what is the defining measure of achievement? In other words, why is achievement valuable? To prosper? To grow? It can be, but only if we take the time to examine the impact of our efforts. Just because you're driving at full speed does not mean you're going in the right direction.

The next time you cross off a Task in your BuJo, slow down. Take a moment to pause and reflect on the impact of your accomplishment. What do you feel? If by chance you feel nothing—or maybe nothing but relief—then chances are the thing you're working so diligently toward isn't adding much value to your life. That's a critical insight that needs to be recognized. If on the other hand you feel even a small sense of joy, pride, appreciation, or fulfillment, then you may be onto something. Gift yourself a moment to appreciate your accomplishment and acknowledge it, because it's trying to reveal something to you. After all, if you can't appreciate your achievements, then what's the point?!

Your achievements have the power to nurture and guide you, but in order for that to happen, you need to take time to be grateful for them.

IN PRACTICE

CELEBRATION

Your Bullet Journal houses a running list of your Tasks. Once complete, a Task turns into an accomplishment. When crossing something off as complete, you're given an opportunity to acknowledge this accomplishment. If its impact is even remotely positive, celebrate it! If it's a big win, such as completing a milestone or a long-term goal, plan a proper celebration, ideally with those who were involved or are excited for your win. If it's a medium-size achievement, maybe call a friend or call it a day a little earlier than usual. If it's a small achievement, smile! Snap your fingers! Do a fist pump. Exclaim: "Done!" Enjoy the dopamine rush. Celebrating your victories isn't just about patting yourself on the back; it trains you to identify positive moments, which allows you to discover—and enjoy—more of them.

Celebrating small wins can produce dramatic improvements in our self-perception and attitude. We tend to ruminate over all the things we got wrong, unaware of or ignoring all the things we got right. By celebrating our accomplishments, we're forcing ourselves to acknowledge our abilities and witness the proof that we can contribute. It shifts our attitude away from "How am I going to get all of this done?" to "Look at all the things I've done! I've got this." The fear of failure will find less purchase in your mind. This is not a self-indulgence. It's an intentional means to build momentum, optimism, and resilience. A simple yet meaningful way to begin appreciating your achievements is to write them down. Committing them to paper makes you pause and honor a good moment with your attention. In the Bullet Journal, you can do this by logging Events that you're grateful for in your Daily Log, in your Monthly Calendar, or in a Gratitude Log.

GRATITUDE PRACTICE

Studies show that we need about five compliments to balance out every negative remark made toward us. That's because we remember negative events more intensely than positive ones. Introducing a gratitude practice—a simple process of regularly taking stock of what you're grateful for—is a good way to counteract your negativity bias by fostering an awareness of the positive things in your life.[46]

Having a gratitude practice has been shown to improve relationships, physical and mental health, empathy, self-esteem, lowering aggression—the list goes on.[47] I like to think of it as helping our ongoing dialogue with life remain productive. With that in mind, let's take a look at two simple examples of how to incorporate a gratitude practice in your Bullet Journal.

1. In your Daily Log (page 86), during your PM Reflection (page 136), write down more than one thing that you're grateful for. Try to do this every day.

2. Create a "Gratitude" Collection (and remember to add it to your Index). Again, write down more than one thing that you're grateful for. Try to do this every day. If you're so

inclined, you can even get creative with how you capture your favorite moments (page 10).

Chances are you'll find yourself quickly running out of obvious things to be grateful for, such as health, home, family, friends, dogs, etc. The trick is to avoid repurposing the things you've listed before. That's when things get interesting. It's when we exhaust our stock answers that we begin to dig into our daily experience for material. It helps us become more present. As you actively examine your experience to find the good, you become better at locating it and appreciating it. You learn that—to paraphrase the Benedictine monk David Steindl-Rast—you can't be grateful for everything, but you can be grateful in every moment.[48]

Even on the days when not much has moved forward, your gratitude practice will help you find things to appreciate—whether it's a coworker who helped you out, a stranger who opened a door, a meal you savored, or a parking space close to the entrance. It will help you remain aware of the things that make life a little more enjoyable. Every day, once a day, give yourself the present of savoring the good in your life.

Gratitude

Mark

the rain gave me a break!

analog tools

POSITIVE COMMENTS ♡

lisa AND bonnie!

#OMIMBJ

TAKING A ME DAY!

Peloton

FEELING healthy

long hot baths

NAPS

CREATIVE TIME

REST

Cream Ridge Veterinary Clinic

ENERGY

baby fever

PUPPY SNUGGLES

hubby

SUNNY DAYS

TACOS!

BELLA ♡

getting BACK TO normal

being self-employed

Gratitude Log by Kara Benz

CONTROL

God, grant me the serenity to accept the things I
cannot change; courage to change the things I can;
and wisdom to know the difference.

—Reinhold Niebuhr

The fact that all things must change is one of the few universal truths. On the one hand it frightens us because things can change for the worse. We invest immense amounts of time and energy, not to mention money, trying to prevent or mitigate negative change like losing our jobs, status, security, health, or relationships. The same is true for implementing positive change, be it our education, appearance, ability, or general personal growth. In both cases, a lot of that effort goes to waste, because it's applied to things we simply have no power to change. Knowing what we can change begins with defining what's in our control.

This endeavor is found at the heart of Stoicism, an ancient school of philosophy focused on cracking the age-old conundrum of how to live a good life. To Stoics, a critical part of the solution was "to know the difference" between the things we can and can't control.

According to them, we can't control the world around us, nor the people in it. It's our futile resistance to this truth that can leave us frustrated, devastated, or at a total loss. For example, when we seek the approval or acknowledgment of others as reward for our efforts, more often than not we're left wanting or downright angry and confused when we don't get what we're looking for. Why are we feeling so bad? Because we've set an expectation for something that isn't in our control.

When you look at life through this lens, a lot of examples come to light. No matter how kind you are to someone, they just don't like you. You provide sound advice, and your friend goes right out and does the opposite. You put in a ton of overtime, only to get passed over for promotion. You open up your heart, and it gets broken. The list, if we let it, can be endless. The more we try to control others, the more draining life becomes.

If we can't control the world or people around us, all we're left with is the world within us, right? Well, we're complex emotional creatures. We can't help but feel anger toward those who wrong us or sadness at a loss. So, no, we're not entirely in control of ourselves, either. Bottom line: We can't control our feelings, people, or external events. But there is something we *can* control, and it's powerful.

*We can control how we respond
to what happens to us.*

It's within our power to be intentional about how we respond to the wildly creative problems the world, people, and even our emotions subject us to. No matter what happens in your life, no matter how bad things get, you're never entirely at the mercy of your experience. There is always opportunity and freedom to be found in how we choose to act. It's our obligation, then, to make the most of this freedom.

> If my computer so much as hiccupped, I'd take it out on my mouse and keyboard in awful ways, which is like punching a puddle to lash out at the rain. When I started Bullet Journaling, I began asking "Why?" before getting upset about every little thing. If someone cut me off on the freeway, I'd ask myself why I'd get upset about something I can't control. Now I just allow more space between my car and the one in front of me.
>
> —Bullet Journalist Trey Kauffman

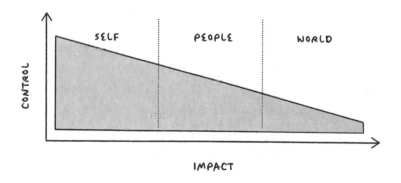

IN PRACTICE

RESPONDING VS. REACTING

Our reactions are often more instinctual than intentional, especially when a situation or a person is doing their best to bring out our worst. Say your colleague Chad offends you and you puff up like a blowfish trying to protect yourself. You could waste so much time contemplating the many ways in which Chad is wrong about you, about the situation, about his choice in shoes, and about life in general. Or worse, you lash out at him, he lashes back, and it spirals down from there until you're both on the same low rung of the evolutionary ladder.

We waste our energy trying to "protect" ourselves because, deep inside, we're animals. When our ancestors were triggered, they survived by running or biting. Fight or flight. Some time has passed since we swung from trees, and we now have other options available to us. We can do better.

Rather than gently ushering Chad out the window, take a deep breath and don't take the bait. Let the heat of the moment pass. During your Daily Reflection, you can start to examine the experience from a better place. Why did he say or do what he did? Why would he volunteer this questionable opinion? Why did it upset you exactly? What are your options here?

Use these thoughts to formulate a measured response in the form of a letter written in your Bullet Journal. Now, to be clear, this letter is not necessarily for Chad. It's for you to get your thoughts straight. It's to reveal opportunities and insights that may have been obscured in the heat of the moment. This trick has helped me deal with very challenging people and situations. First of all, it allows you to safely vent. Getting it all out of your head offers some much needed relief. Seeing your thoughts on paper can also highlight where you're being petty, unreasonable, or even irrational. With that out of the way, you can begin to dial it back, restating your case in a calm considered way, and to figure out productive next steps.

For example, it might hit you that a main source of contention is that you don't understand where the other person is coming from. You can probably get clarity on that. If you're able to have a conversation with the other person, try to actually hear what they're saying. You may realize that they have a point. Perhaps they misperceived something, and if you were in their place, you would be angry also. The fact that they acted like a ding-dong doesn't make them wrong . . . and just because you were offended does not make you right.

In the process of writing this letter, perhaps you realize what they said or did has nothing to do with you. In the heat of a challenging moment, it's easy to forget that our assailant may be struggling with their own measure of pain. By reacting with fear or anger, we only deepen their wounds and ours, severing opportunities for understanding, progress, or resolution. We also prolong wasting time and energy worrying about something that we can't control.

PROCESS VS. OUTCOME

Mark Twain once wrote, "I've had a lot of worries in my life, most of which never happened."[49] Worry has a way of holding our attention hostage. This is especially true for things we can't control due to the elevated level of uncertainty. We burn through a lot of resources obsessing over possible outcomes and forming contingency plans, but in reality we're just fueling our anxiety. Trying to think our way out of situations beyond our control may feel productive, but it's nothing more than a powerful distraction.

> *Worry baits us with the promise of a solution*
> *but usually offers none.*

As the Dalai Lama once said: "If a problem can be solved, there is no use worrying about it. If it can't be solved, worrying will do no good."[50]

During your Daily Reflection, or Monthly Migration, scan your Tasks and try to identify what is and what is not in your control. An easy tell is if your tasks are focused on outcome rather than process: "• Give awesome presentation," "• Lose 10 pounds," "• Read five books," or "• Get Chad to see reason" are goals. Though goals provide direction, they focus on outcomes that are ultimately out of our control. This is why we break our goals down into small actionable steps: "• Memorize presentation," "• No soda on Sunday," "• Set aside reading time," and "• Address Chad's concerns." These are the things you can control.

By identifying what is out of our control and letting go, we can reclaim our attention and reinvest it into the things that are. Focus on doing everything within your control to help something succeed. There is nothing more that can be asked of us. More importantly, there is nothing more that we can ask of ourselves.

RADIANCE

*As a man changes his own nature, so does the attitude
of the world change towards him.*

—Mahatma Gandhi

Think about a toxic colleague you've worked with. Though you may be pretty content with your job, what does it feel like when they bad-mouth the company, complain about their work, or manipulate people to get what they want? It leaves a bad taste in your mouth; it stays with you. Without even realizing it, you can spread that negativity to your partner over dinner, and even to your *partner's* colleagues the next day, one study found.[51]

Like a pebble dropped into a lake, our actions ripple out into the world around us. Each ripple influences what it encounters, which in turn ripples out even farther. When you hold the door open for someone, for example, it may inspire a willingness for them to do so for the next person or to extend a different kindness that would not have existed without your influence. Similarly, when you snap at someone, chances are their spouse, friend, or child will be subject to the ripple effects of your action. I like to refer to this ability of ours to influence the world around us as our radiance—literally, what we radiate.

The nature of our radiance is often a reflection of what's going on inside. It's why cultivating self-awareness, far from being selfish, is vitally important. If we remain unaware of (or unwilling to) take responsibility for our lesser qualities, such as negativity or anger, we will inevitably pass them on to those in our proximity. The charge of your words or actions begins to shape the world around you to parallel the one within. Your lack of enthusiasm for a project drains the team of theirs. Watch your bad mood be served back to you in the silence of your partner over dinner.

I'm not suggesting that you force yourself to become a chirpy Disney character with rainbows of perpetual optimism blasting out your nose. Rather, we have an obligation to address our weaknesses and to build on our strengths because we're not alone. Cultivating our potential makes us more valuable to ourselves *and* to others, especially those closest to us.

Though you can't control people, you will in some way *influence* those you come in contact with, and they in turn may carry forward that influence. Your knowledge can teach others. Your hard work can inspire others. Your positive mood can uplift others. Seth Godin once wrote, "You're either the person who creates energy. Or you're the one who destroys it."[52]

Bettering yourself leads to bettering others and—if we play that ripple effect all the way out to its infinite potential and multiply it by every willing soul—to bettering the world. If you don't want to become better for yourself, do it for them. If your goal in life is to be useful to others, you can start by figuring out how to be useful to yourself.

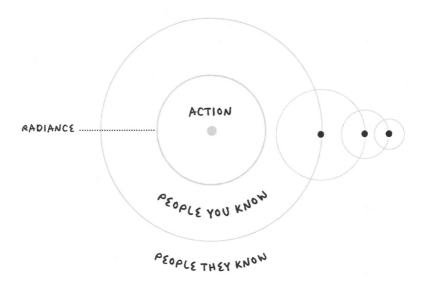

IN PRACTICE

SELF-COMPASSION

Take a moment to think of a friend who is going through a rough patch. Maybe they messed up at work or were cruel to someone or just got dumped. Whatever it is, they're feeling pretty lousy about themselves. You probably patiently sat there and listened to them fixate on all the ways in which they are a terrible or useless person.

Maybe you tried to correct their distorted self-perception. You pointed out the things they do well and the things they do right. You reminded them how much you care about them and that everyone makes mistakes. Perhaps you tried suggesting a way forward, because you know that dwelling on perceived failures or shortcomings is entirely unhelpful. At the very least, you listened. We're happy to offer support and solace to those we care for. What if we extended this same kindness to ourselves?

Easier said than done, right? We can find countless reasons to be hard on ourselves, especially if we are insecure, are sensitive, or breathe. We need to start trading in browbeating for the same clear-eyed, compassionate counsel that we'd offer to others.

Self-compassion can start by asking yourself
a simple question: What would I tell
a friend in this situation?

Asking this question interrupts our inner critic and makes us switch gears into problem-solving mode. Can you imagine if a tormented friend came to you for help and all you did was exacerbate their suffering? Of course you can't, because you're a good friend and you care. Yet that's exactly what many of us do to ourselves all the time.

The next time you find yourself beating up the person who blows out your birthday candles, pretend that you're taking care of a friend in need. What patient and compassionate advice would you offer to help them overcome or recontextualize their situation? If they messed up at work, for example, it could tip off a downward spiral where they start questioning their ability, their worth, and so on. They quickly lose perspective. One simple way to make them feel better is to present evidence that would force them to question their inner critic. We can use the same tactic when we face our own.

When we've erred, the voice of our inner critic grows loud, and it can be most convincing. Luckily we have some pretty compelling evidence to prove them wrong, and it's penned in our own hand! If you've been using your Daily Log, you've recorded clear examples of your success, ability, kindness, caring, etc. This is especially true if you're keeping a Gratitude Log (page 183). Whatever it is that you may be faulting yourself for, it's likely that you'll find inarguable proof to the contrary within the pages of your Bullet Journal.

When you're down, look at these examples during your Reflections. Show yourself the evidence, and allow yourself to accept it. It may be hard, and you may remain skeptical at first, but try to make room in the dark inner choir for a benevolent voice. The longer that voice remains, the more opportunities it has to be heard. Over time, you may just be willing to trust it.

MUTUAL IMPROVEMENT

Radiance is a two-way street. So be mindful about the people you surround yourself with, because they *will* shape you. Their strengths and weaknesses can have a tremendous influence on your own trajectory. It's critical therefore to be deliberate about who you cultivate relationships with, both professionally and personally.

Look through your Bullet Journal to see who you're spending your time with. You may know how you feel about them, but have you ever considered their impact on you? Start to take notes on some of these interactions. Don't worry, you're not keeping creepy records on your friends; you're simply becoming mindful of how their radiance affects you. Add some notes about the dinner, date, or meeting when you get home. Did you have fun? What did you learn? Was most of your time spent just sitting there listening to their problems . . . again? How do you feel when you're with them? You can quickly capture it like this:

○ **Dinner with Becca @ Evelina's**
   - Talked about aspirations
   - Want to travel to Portugal together
   - Want to co-host the next party
   - Always leave feeling motivated after we hang out

It may seem awkward at first, but recording your interactions grants you the opportunity to articulate something you may not have otherwise. You never know what it could reveal. Maybe you realize that the relationship is vampiric: It often leaves you feeling drained. Or that it's one-sided: You always call and put in all the work. In contrast, you may realize that some people leave you feeling inspired, lighter, energized, contemplative, or calmer. Whatever the case may be, you're becoming more aware so you can be intentional about managing your relationships, including which relationships are worth managing at all.

Negative or unmotivated people in your life may sabotage your efforts to live with intention. Try to keep company with those you find inspiring, motivating, and constructively challenging. Ask yourself: *What can I learn from them? Is the world a bit of a better place because they're in my life? Do they make me want to be a better person?*

As Joshua Fields Millburn of the Minimalists once quipped, "You can't change the people around you, but you can change the people around you."[53] You get to choose who you spend your precious time with. Surround yourself with people who want the best for you. That doesn't mean they'll always agree with you or be indiscriminately supportive. No, find people who want you to succeed, even if that means having hard conversations, disagreeing with you, and telling you when you're wrong or being unreasonable. We all need to be checked from time to time. Find people who challenge you to grow from a place of mutual respect, appreciation, and caring.

LEARNING

The best way for your radiance to serve others is to challenge yourself to grow. To that end, make deliberate learning an ongoing focus of your life. Being intentional in your pursuit of knowledge will help you engage with the world and open it up in ways you would have never considered, or been willing to, otherwise.

During your Reflections, ask yourself:

— *What am I learning?*
— *What lessons has _____ [situation or relationship] taught me or inspired me to learn?*
— *What do I want to know more about? How will I go about learning it?*

Whether it's reading, classes, conversations with trusted friends and mentors, or enriching experiences, make it part of your plans. Use your Bullet Journal to identify the things that inspire further inquiry. Once you know what grabs your interest, set your goals (page 150). You can tackle them the same way you would any other goal in the Bullet Journal, but I've also provided the following visual example of how to apply this approach directly to learning.

With each thing you learn, you become a more capable, well-rounded, substantive individual. You'll add more value to anyone within your presence—not because of what you do for them, but because of what you've done to illuminate yourself.

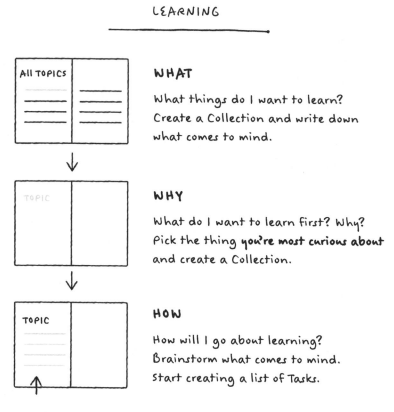

LEARNING

WHAT

What things do I want to learn?
Create a Collection and write down
what comes to mind.

WHY

What do I want to learn first? Why?
Pick the thing you're most curious about
and create a Collection.

HOW

How will I go about learning?
Brainstorm what comes to mind.
Start creating a list of Tasks.

Ask yourself, what small thing can I
do now to get this process started?
Maybe it's figuring out a time to
research. Get to it!

ENDURANCE

If you know the why, you can live any how.
—FRIEDRICH NIETZSCHE

I don't know about you, but I deeply hate doing dishes. It's stupid, I know. I've tried to make it a mindfulness practice, a way to unplug, but no. It was my boyhood chore for years, and that soured the deed for the rest of time.

My partner at the time wanted to learn how to cook. Developing that skill forced me to spend my nights begrudgingly bulldozing the ectoplasm off our kitchenware. And so it went. She would come home, quickly undo my culinary exorcism from the previous evening.

Yes, I should've just been grateful that I was getting home-cooked meals, especially after she worked hard all day, but I petulantly resented spending my limited free time cleaning up meal after meal.

All of that changed one night when I heard her sing.

She was going through a really hard time when she took up cooking. Her usually vibrant and charmingly goofy personality, which had drawn me to her in the first place, was dialed way down.

Our communication was usually strong, but whatever she was going through was something I couldn't help with. Of course, that added to my frustration. After all, when the ones we love are in pain, the last thing we want to do is nothing.

One night, before dinner, I was lifted from my work by a soft melody that floated through our flat. I didn't understand what was happening, as I had *never* heard her sing in the years we had been together. But there she was, quietly singing and swaying by the stove, fixing us supper.

That's when it dawned on me. This whole cooking thing had nothing to do with food at all. It was her way of battling her demons while still showing me how much she cared. It was something she could control. That night while I did the dishes, that peaceful image of her wouldn't leave my mind. I realized that all I had to do to help her—all that I could do—was get my hands wet.

As time went on, she got better. I began looking forward to her meals as she slowly eased back into her lovely old self. In fact, these dinners became a safe place that allowed us to deepen our relationship. When things got rocky and we needed to have a talk, one of us would cook a meal for the other. No matter how hard the conversation, it was always accompanied by this loving effort, a sign of deep respect and caring. That included doing the dishes—which, it turns out, was her least favorite thing to do, too. Nothing deepens a relationship more than something you can hate together.

Did all this make me enjoy doing the dishes? No, but it did allow me to see how it mattered. This seemingly menial chore that I had merely endured suddenly added real value to my life. What had changed? Not the pedestrian process of washing dishes. Of course, what had changed was me. This task began to matter to me, and I tried harder. One day she walked by while I was cleaning up after the best meal I've ever enjoyed, and she kissed me on the cheek and said, "Thank you. I know it was a lot tonight and that you hate doing this, but it really helps me. It makes me feel loved."

When I used to think about defining and finding what mattered—what was truly meaningful to me—it seemed to require some dramatic gesture. Perhaps I'd have to pack my bags and seek out an enlightened cave dweller in a cold, remote corner of the earth. I know now that meaning can be found much closer to home.

Meaning can reveal itself in the most unremarkable, unpredictable, and quiet of moments. If we're not listening to the world around us, as well as the one within, we may miss it—the music in the mundane. This is a skill that can be acquired through study— but not of academics or anything beyond our ken. The subject of our study is our experience.

Often we operate unconsciously. We make our way through life on autopilot, seldom stopping to understand why something makes us feel the way it does. Without personal context, without understanding how something adds value to your life, your efforts will ultimately feel meaningless. Context helps us understand how some unpleasant or even painful responsibilities actually benefit us. Let's explore some ways to surface context.

IN PRACTICE

CLARITY LOG

Sam Cawthorn, founder of Speakers Tribe, once said, "The happiest people don't necessarily have the best of everything, but they make the most of everything."[54] A powerful way to begin this process is to reframe the mundane in our mind. Many Tasks may not inspire much joy at first blush: Do the laundry, finish project, buy groceries, etc. Rather than focusing on the drudgery of the action, spend a moment focusing on the experiences they enable. Doing the laundry gives you fluffy towels after your shower, fresh shirts for your workday, and crisp sheets to slip between at night. Finishing a project gives you a feeling of satisfaction of a job well done and keeps that paycheck rolling in—maybe some of which is going toward your Hawaii vacation (page 252). Buying groceries will put a tasty meal on your table or allow you to spend some quality time with your loved ones.

This is not about positive thinking; it's about systematically analyzing your efforts to define their purpose. We don't tend to contextualize our obligations this way. To help us become mindful of *why* we're doing *what* we're doing, we can create a "Clarity Log" in our Bullet Journal. Scan your Daily Logs and identify the obligations or chores that you struggle with the most. Take one and write it down on the left page of your Clarity Log. Let's take paying rent, for example:

Paying rent bums me out because it feels like a waste of money.

Sure, it's easy to look at paying rent as the monthly ritual where you shovel your hard-won living into the icy void where your landlord's soul should be. But surely there was a reason you rented the place. Let's balance our negative perception of this obligation by taking a moment to focus on what you enjoy about your home.

Close your eyes and conjure a detail or two about what keeps you there, what makes this space a home. Whatever it is, write it on the facing page, across from the challenge:

- The way that shaft of light warms the floor by the bed in the morning
- The fragrance of the coffee shop wafting in through the windows
- The commute time

No place is perfect, but if you're mostly happy with your home, then paying rent can be reframed as the act of rewarding yourself every month with those joys. It clarifies why this seeming chore is meaningful.

Another way to discover personal meaning is to consider those we love. Perhaps this exercise made you realize that you truly don't like your home (if so, I apologize; I've been there). Not all is lost. Think about why you moved there through the lens of your relationships. Maybe this home allowed your kids to go to a better school. Maybe it allowed you to be closer to work, so you would spend less time commuting and more time with friends. Whatever it was, write it down.

Connecting your obligations to the people you love can inject them with much-needed meaning. While it may not make these responsibilities any more enjoyable, it does finally give them purpose, which can make even the most onerous task more bearable.

CLARITY LOG

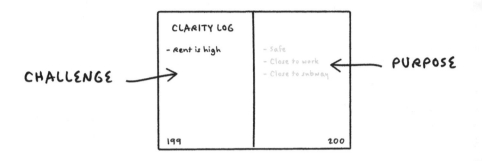

TRACK PROGRESS

What if you've tried this exercise but failed to find the benefit or meaning underlying some obligation? Many things we do don't immediately reveal their value. Meaning, much like a terrible guest, often arrives late, bearing a great bottle of wine. Observant patience is the key.

If you're failing to find the purpose of a particular pursuit, keep an eye on it. Monthly Migration can also be used to monitor progress. Use it as a milestone to check in with yourself to see if anything has shifted.

If you finally come to the conclusion that an obligation is adding no value to your life, or that the effort far outweighs the value it provides, then you've identified a distraction. Let it go. If you can't let it go for whatever reason, deconstruct (page 209) your obligation and figure out your alternatives.

DECONSTRUCTION

What stands in the way becomes the way.

—MARCUS AURELIUS

One of the oldest texts known to us is the Enûma Eliš. It's a Babylonian creation myth that pits Marduk, champion of the gods, against Tiamat, a dragon-like beast, mother to monsters, who is determined to destroy the gods. It depicts an epic battle to the death between good and evil, order and chaos. Marduk slays Tiamat and then proceeds to dismember her body, using the pieces to lay the foundation for all of creation. Her ribs become the sky, and her mouth becomes the ocean. Though a bit ghastly, it's a powerful metaphor for how we can deconstruct our challenges and use them to our advantage.

When I graduated from college, I was fortunate to get the internship of my dreams. I double majored in graphic design and creative writing, and I wanted to combine these skills by working on title sequences. You know, those micro movies that bookend the actual film? The internship was working for a man who was pioneering the resurgence of this art form and whose work was greatly inspiring.

I moved to New York with two bags and took up residence in a mildewy basement apartment I could hardly afford, with two room-mates who nabbed the good rooms and a jumpy cat I didn't see eye to eye with. It was a small price to pay for my new career.

The week before I was scheduled to start, I called the office to get the final details about the internship. It turned out that because of the World Trade Center attacks the year before, the company had downsized. Long story short, I had been laid off before my first day, and no one had even bothered to tell me. Suddenly I found myself just another unemployed art student in New York, searching for work in one of the bleakest job markets in recent history, during one of the harshest winters in decades.

For many months, I looked fruitlessly for a job. My meager sav-ings evaporated. On good days, I'd trudge through snow, jam my portfolio into packed subway cars at rush hour, and thaw while being interrogated, I mean, interviewed by a bored HR staffer for some job I was inevitably unqualified for. On bad days, I just sat in front of the computer applying for any job I could find.

One morning I woke up to a strange sound. I opened my eyes and noticed the floor was moving—no, the floor was under water! The snow had melted overnight and had pooled in my bedroom. Floating by my bed was my portfolio, filled with my design work that I was using to apply for jobs. My first thought was: *At least it's all backed up.* That's when I saw my backup drive submerged on the floor, and my computer flickering next to it. That morning, I lost nearly everything I owned.

Shortly thereafter, I accepted the first job I was offered purely to survive. The job had nothing at all to do with my skill set, but I was broke and homeless.

In my first week I learned that my predecessors had all run away screaming, and it quickly dawned on me why. My main function was to compile backlist order forms, lists of all the books that this company had published . . . hundreds of thousands of them. Yes, I'm into lists, but this was a special kind of hell even for me.

There was no solid tech or system to facilitate this process, so inevitably something somewhere would go wrong and all inky fingers would point at me. On top of all this, I reported to a wildly abusive boss who systematically dismantled any confidence or self-worth I had. She screamed at me so loudly once that people from adjacent offices came running in because they thought there was a "situation." It got to the point where I was actually afraid to go to work. I didn't know how, but something had to change.

Once again, I started interviewing for any position I could find. It did not go well. The truth was, I had nothing to show for myself. My portfolio was gone, I had a few random summer internships' worth of experience, and I was working a job mostly unrelated to my skill set. *I* wouldn't have hired me! I swallowed my pride and accepted the fact that I had to make myself more valuable.

In my proto Bullet Journal, I started mapping out how I was spending my free time. A fair amount of it was spent online. I started tracking what I was spending my time looking at and realized that I was reading and learning about interactive online experiences. There was a nascent movement of experimental websites mixing art, photography, video, and design into fascinating interactive narratives. It was also around the time that personal websites started popping up, especially for artists, designers, and small businesses.

Still recovering from the flood, I could deeply appreciate the benefits of having my work online, far removed from the clutches of negligent landlords and wet acts of god. Also, it so happened that several friends had asked if I could build websites for them or the businesses they worked for. Perhaps there would be some money in it?

I scraped together whatever remained of my laughable salary and started taking night classes in the then-new field of "web design." A couple of nights a week, I dragged myself to the windowless classroom, exhausted from my day job, but motivated. For the first time in a long time, I was working on something that resonated with me. I learned how to design and code rudimentary websites. I jumped at any opportunity that presented itself. First I designed a site for a local restaurant, then another for the restaurant's bartender's band, and so on. Eventually I was able to scrape up just enough freelance work to resign and fully focus on an entirely new career path.

While I can't say I charted this path skillfully or even particularly willingly, the experience taught me that it's all too easy to start feeling as if we're being held hostage by our circumstances. Be they taxes, paying rent, taking care of a sick family member, or paying off student loans, these are the dragons in our lives. We can cower in fear, rage against fate, play the martyr, wallow in self-pity, waiting for the skies to magically part and be rescued—or we can take up arms.

IN PRACTICE

We have a tendency to blow our problems way out of proportion. No matter how bad a problem really is, chances are we're making it much worse in our minds. It can feel all-consuming, making us believe we're powerless, and helpless, but that's never true. No matter how bleak or menacing a situation may appear, it does not entirely own us. It can't take away our freedom to respond, our power to take action.

Even the smallest action can start changing our circumstances. The first action can be simply pausing to examine your problem so you can begin to deconstruct it. To do this, we'll use a technique known as the Five Whys.

THE FIVE WHYS

Sakichi Toyoda, founder of Toyota and father of the Japanese industrial revolution, invented this technique to uncover the causes of technical problems in his company's manufacturing process. It's a deceptively simple method to unearth root issues and expose unexpected opportunities. It does this by breaking down a seemingly large problem into its individual components.

We can use the same approach for tackling our challenges using our Bullet Journals. Start a new Collection and give it a Topic that names the problem: "I can't pay rent." Now ask yourself *why*. Write down the answer. Now, challenge your answer by asking *why* again. Do the same for the next answer, and so on, up to five times.

I CAN'T PAY RENT.

1. Why? Because I don't have the money.
2. Why? Because the rent is high.
3. Why? Because I live in a nice area.
4. Why? Because I like living there.
5. Why? Because the neighborhood has nice people, good shops and restaurants, and makes me feel safe.

We've now deconstructed one large challenge into its smaller components, each of which we can target separately. More importantly, in this example, we also surfaced the underlying values being threatened by this situation. Often, when deconstructing a challenge, you'll discover what's truly at stake. In this case, it's not really about the rent; it's about losing the feeling of pleasure and safety. These are two important data points that can be used to inform your plan of attack.

PLAN OF ATTACK

With our list of reasons clearly laid out, the next step is to figure out what our options are. Naturally, this is done by creating another list. You can do this on the facing page of your "I can't pay rent" Collection.

If the issue is that you don't have the money, you can start listing ways you could tackle that specific issue. A few that come to mind are:

1. Ask for a raise.
2. Look for a better-paying job.
3. Get a roommate.
4. Move to a different neighborhood where the cost of living is lower.
5. Take continuing education classes to increase your value.

Now we're making some progress! Each entry is a path forward. Now, with your options clearly laid out before you, pick the one that excites you the most—the one that shines forth.

Let's say you chose "Take continuing education classes to increase your value." That's your goal. Flip to the next blank spread and create a Subcollection dedicated to this goal. With your goal set up, break it down into actionable steps like research fields of interest, find different schools offering classes, sign up for a class, and so on. This is your plan of attack. Each Task you complete is a successful blow landed in the battle with your dragon.

Life is full of dragons. The longer they live, the bigger they become, feeding off our misfortunes, resentments, and sense of helplessness. Stare them down. Look directly into their big, terrible eyes. There, you will see your own reflection. Our challenges are mirrors, exposing our vulnerabilities, insecurities, weaknesses, and fears. As hard as it may be, don't turn away. See them, examine them, meet your fears with curiosity, and you will discover a way forward. It's entirely possible that your courage will be rewarded with opportunities for personal or professional growth that would have been hidden from you otherwise.

In my case, my dragon was my job. It terrified me. It embodied all the things I had naively sworn never to subject myself to: a dead-end job that was not creative in any meaningful way. But I had to pay my bills, so I took it. I was so caught up in my own misery that I forgot a simple truth: As long as our hearts are beating, there is always opportunity.

Finally, after another particularly savage verbal abuse session from my boss, I'd had enough. I was tired of being a victim, not only to her, but also to my lesser qualities. I was tired of being the honored (and only) guest at my personal pity party, tired of the feeling of helplessness. These miseries were entirely my own doing, as if enduring this terrible situation made me some kind of a noble martyr. It was ridiculous and immature. I was just trying to ignore the fact that the only solution would have to come from me, and no one else.

It started with setting a goal: Get a new job. When I realized that that was not going to happen because I didn't have anything to show for myself, I simply set a new goal: Learn to build websites.

That's when I started using my dragon—my job—against itself. My meager salary paid for classes. The abuse and meaninglessness of my position motivated me to drag myself to night school. As hard as it was, each class felt like a little victory in my battle. Finally, I was able to land my killing blow, not with a sword, but with a terse letter of resignation printed on paper warped by the flood.

Now when things are not going my way, or when I need to work on something that doesn't inspire me to do backflips, I think back to my Tiamat. I look around and see all the things that I was able to make from that experience. It forced me to learn how to code, which led to a fulfilling career as a digital product designer, which provided the hands-on education I needed to launch Bulletjournal .com, which ultimately resulted in the privilege to write this book and share the Bullet Journal with you.

INERTIA

I shall either find a way or make one.
—HANNIBAL BARCA

In the chapter on Goals (page 150), we talked about breaking down major challenges into smaller, more manageable Sprints. But what happens if you get stuck along the way? Maybe you're hung up on a problem, or you've lost motivation, or you're having a hard time finding a way forward on a project, goal, or in a relationship. Whatever the reason may be, you're left feeling frustrated by the sense of inertia. What to do? Here are two techniques I've found very useful in getting back some traction.

IN PRACTICE

RUBBER DUCKING

A friend who is a successful small business owner was looking to open another location. She applied for a loan to finance the buildout of the new space. Though she already ran three profitable branches, the bank turned down her request. Understandably upset, she called her accountant and started walking him through the problem. Piece by piece she began articulating what she was trying to accomplish. As she did so, she began to realize that her goal wasn't so much about opening this specific location as it was about growing her business. She opted to create five small pop-up shops to test which location would bring in the most business. This she could afford without any outside support. She figured out a solution by explaining the problem.

This process is known as rubber ducking, which originates from the book *The Pragmatic Programmer* by Andrew Hunt and David Thomas. The authors tell the story of a developer who solves problems in their code by explaining them line by line to a rubber duck. Yes, I'm talking about the small yellow bath toy.

We're apt to lose our objectivity when we're spinning our wheels. By explaining a problem in detail to someone (or something) else, we're forced to change our perspective, viewing it from above, so to speak, and not from the depths of whatever mental hole we've dug ourselves into.

If no one's around to listen, you can sit down with your Bullet Journal and write a letter to "Dear Duck"—or some other benign, trusted, or accepting entity. Tell them about:

— Your problem
— What's not working
— Why it isn't working
— What you've tried
— What you have not tried yet
— What you want to have happen

The important part is getting it out of your head. Craft your explanation with care and patience. Do so with the understanding that this entity may not have all the information that you do. Good communication bridges the gap between information and understanding. In the process of carefully communicating the problem, you may help yourself figure out a solution. And if a letter to your rubber duck, padded panda, stupid stapler, or, God forbid, Chad doesn't do the trick, we can try something else . . .

BREAK-SPRINTS

If you've been following along in sequence, at this point you should have a "Goals" Collection set up. This Collection can serve as a powerful inspirational resource when you're feeling stuck or unmotivated. I know, I know, I had mentioned earlier not to revisit your "Goals" Collection until you're done with the ones you're working on, but this is an emergency! When you're really stuck or out of ideas, it usually means that you've lost perspective. You may no longer be able to see a way forward because you're too close to the subject. To regain some perspective, it can help to temporarily disengage your mind by focusing on something else. To that end, we'll create what I like to call a break-sprint.

Much like the Sprints (page 157) we covered earlier in the book, break-sprints are self-contained micro projects. They're designed for the sole purpose of helping your mind get unstuck. A break-sprint can be set up in your Bullet Journal the same way as a standard Sprint, but it follows a subtly different set of rules:

1. **It should take two weeks or less to complete.** You need a break, but you don't want to lose the thread of your main project.

2. **It should be unrelated to the project/problem that's troubling you.** You and your main project need space. You're not breaking up, but you're taking some much-needed "me time."

3. **Very critically, it needs to have a defined end (and a clear beginning and middle, too).** When we feel stuck, our sense of inertia drains our motivation. One goal of your break-sprint is to give you the satisfaction of crossing off the final Task, of feeling that sense of accomplishment and closure. Reminding yourself what that feels like can quickly refuel your drive.

BREAK-SPRINT "PARE DOWN CLOTHES"

BREAKING IT DOWN

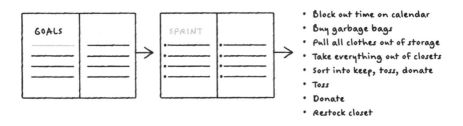

- Block out time on calendar
- Buy garbage bags
- Pull all clothes out of storage
- Take everything out of closets
- Sort into keep, toss, donate
- Toss
- Donate
- Restock closet

Take that online class, write that article, organize your digital photo gallery, KonMari your closet, volunteer with your colleagues. It's entirely up to you. Just make sure it's something you're curious about.

By the end of your break-sprint, you'll have been exposed to something new. You will have used your mind in a different way, to have thoughts you would not have had otherwise. Every new experience helps us grow and grants us new perspective. You'll be ever so slightly different than you were the last time you tried to tackle the challenge that had you feeling stuck, and that can make all the difference.

IMPERFECTION

There is a crack in everything,
that's how the light gets in.

—LEONARD COHEN

The holiday festivities had long passed, leaving the usually crowded New York streets empty. It was as though the city had gone into mass hibernation, bracing itself against the mirthless stretch of winter ahead.

My then-partner and I had been going through a rough patch, so I decided to plan a romantic stay-at-home date night for us. I had tracked down that bottle of wine we'd enjoyed at our favorite place that had since been shuttered. On the menu was handmade sweet potato gnocchi. I had never made it before, but I knew she loved it. How hard could it be?

Turns out, really hard. Naturally everything went comically wrong from the get-go, and I had to start over from scratch . . . a few times. I spent hours baffled by the recipe, my face as contorted as the potatoes. As the hours passed, I grew increasingly irritable and frantic. The image of her coming home to a perfectly dressed table, flickering candles, with music softly playing in the background was going up in smoke.

By the skin of my teeth, I got it done. She walked in, saw the table, dropped all her bags, and jumped into my arms, burying her cold face in my chest. When she looked up at me, her huge smile faded a little and she asked me what was wrong. "Nothing," I replied sullenly, dusting flour off my pants.

We sat down and she went on about how amazing everything was, but I was too busy brooding over all the mistakes I had made preparing the meal. This was undercooked, that was too cold . . . I was comparing what was with what I had hoped would be: that perfect image in my mind. The only thing I failed to see was how enchanted she was by the gesture and how that joy slowly drained as I kept harping on about what I could have done better. I managed to spoil the most important ingredient of the dinner: our time together. All because I wanted everything to be perfect.

Perfection is an unnatural and damaging concept. I say unnatural because as far as I'm able to tell, there is not a single thing in the physical world, when examined closely enough, that fully adheres to our own definition of perfection: that which is faultless and cannot be improved upon. Even our standards of measurement don't comply. For example, the International Prototype of the Kilogram, more affectionately known as Le Grand K (it was created in France), was the physical object that set the standard of one of the most widely used measurements of weight in the world. Duplicates were shipped around the globe for other countries to use as their standard. It turned out that over time these "perfect" objects had individually changed in mass. For a standard of weight, that's a critical problem. After all, a perfect absolute should not be able to change. That's why, these days, such standards are expressed in terms of equations and concepts.

Now you may fire back and say, "What about me getting 100 percent on my math test? That's a perfect score!" Sure, your answers may have been correct, but were the questions? What was the point of the test? Was it a perfect way of assessing your ability? No, tests are approximations at best. There are plenty of people who test well yet perform poorly. There are even more who test poorly but perform well.

One could argue that perfection only exists in the intangible concepts, theories, and beliefs used to define the ideal, the permanent, and the divine. Why am I belaboring this point? Because the idea of perfection all too often sabotages our ability to become who we have the potential to be.

We're marvelous yet imperfect creatures—and few things make this as clear as inventing unattainable standards to hold ourselves to. So our aspirations often wither on the vine because of our inability to live up to the misguided ideals we hold for our bodies, our minds, our achievements, and our relationships.

Failing to be perfect is one of our biggest sources of self-loathing. It's intentionality gone bad, where we spend time and energy undoing our progress. We tear up our plans, recommit to counterproductive behaviors, and empower our inner critic.

The big misconception is that the alternative to perfection is failure. Mercifully, life isn't binary; it exists on a spectrum. On one side, we have the unattainable: perfection. On the opposite side, we find the unavoidable: chaos. All of the beauty that exists in the world hangs in the balance.

In Japan, there is the term *wabi-sabi*. Wabi-sabi posits that the beauty of an object is found *in* its imperfection. In direct contrast to the Western perspective, which tends to conflate perfection with beauty, wabi-sabi celebrates transience, individuality, and the flawed nature of a thing. These are the qualities that make it unique, genuine, and beautiful. The cracks in the pot, the warp in the wood, the leaves on the stone, the spatter of the ink. It mirrors the Buddhist philosophies, in which wisdom comes from making peace with our fallible natures.

Embracing our imperfection puts the emphasis back where it should be: continual improvement. This mind-set turns mistakes from land mines into street signs, pointing us toward where we need to go.

> *By celebrating transience, the universal changing nature of all things, wabi-sabi champions a forgiving path with limitless opportunities to progress.*

IN PRACTICE

PRACTICING IMPERFECTION

Now, you may be thinking, *I'm all too aware of how human I am; I don't need any more practice in imperfection.* It's not about making mistakes on purpose; it's about reframing your response to them. In meditation, the goal, so far as there can be one, is to be present. By disentangling ourselves from our thoughts, we can view them objectively. Easier said than done.

Even the most experienced practitioners are consumed by their thoughts from time to time. The key is realizing that you're stuck in a thought, and pulling yourself back out of it. More so, it's to perceive the wanderings of your mind not as a mistake, but as an opportunity. Each time you come back into the present, you ever so slightly strengthen your ability to focus. In this way, you begin to embrace a flaw with curiosity instead of judgment.

Are you the type of person who strives to have a perfect notebook? Maybe you don't have great handwriting, or you lack the artistic ability to make your notebook pretty. Does that matter? Only if you want it to. You could look at your notebook as the evidence of your imperfections, *or* you could look at it as a testament to your courage. Those crooked lines and rough letters paint a picture of someone striving to learn and make a positive change in their life. It may not be perfect, but it's unquestionably beautiful.

Do you abandon notebooks when you make a mistake or get a false start? If so, try creating an "Imperfection Collection." Somewhere in your notebook, dedicate space where you just. let. go. Maybe start by writing your name with your nondominant hand. Scribble, doodle, whatever you like. Do what you fear would make your notebook feel flawed. Does it make your Bullet Journal any less valuable? No. One could argue that now it's one of a kind. Whenever you find yourself obsessing over getting every little thing perfect, remind yourself it's just a tool. It's what you're building that counts.

By accepting that we can't be perfect and that
we will fail, we can get back to work.

GOOD CHANGE

Isn't self-improvement or personal development striving for perfection?
It depends on the goal you set. Rather than aiming for perfection or striving to be better than others, find opportunities to continually improve yourself. As W. L. Sheldon purportedly wrote: "There is nothing noble in being superior to your fellow man; true nobility is being superior to your former self."

To fully appreciate wabi-sabi as a model for personal growth, it helps to look a little closer at the culture it originated in. The Japanese have a long history of elevating craftsmanship to mystifying levels, be it carpentry, metalsmithing, even product packaging. Great emphasis was placed on mastery rather than on perfection. Mastery, unlike perfection, embraces both transience and imperfection, because it is a process, a state of being, not an end goal. It is the continued result of improvement and learning. Author Malcolm Gladwell, citing Daniel Levitin, famously described the 10,000-hour rule, which states that 10,000 hours of deliberate practice is required to become world-class at anything.[55] Japanese apprenticeships could span a lifetime.

Mastery replaces the notion of perfection with aspiring to better ourselves through dedication and practice. When it comes to skill, there can be no fixed point. Even the greatest masters remain avid students. Their skill, like our own, develops over time. They all started somewhere, and chances are their first efforts were just as clumsy as any of ours would be.

Every day, ask yourself small questions. Figure out some way in which you can improve. Then format the answer as a Task or Goal and log it in your Bullet Journal. Keep track of your progress.

Every action is a step up from where you were. It doesn't matter how small the steps are, or if you stumble along the way. What matters is that you continue to step up.

IV

THE ART

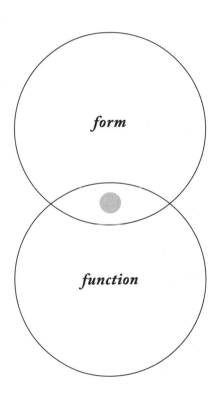

form

function

THE ART

I recently took a terrible capoeira class. For those unfamiliar with the term, capoeira is a martial art invented by Brazilian slaves that cloaked its martial intent behind dance-like movements that mingle acrobatics, contortionism, sing-along, and the tightly wound intensity of tango. When "playing," two capoeiristas fluidly whirl around each other's bodies, often deploying gravity-defying handstands and flips. The modern break-dancers and urban runners whose videos you can see on YouTube liberally appropriate movements from capoeira. In short, it's an impressive and bewildering thing to behold, and more than a little mind- and body-bending to do.

I sloshed my way through a tropical downpour to get to the leaky jungle hangar where the class was being held. Only four of us washed up in the rain—yours truly, one other student, and two very stoned capoeira teachers. They mumbled through some introduction and asked us if we had any experience. My fellow student admitted she had never heard of capoeira before that morning. The not-so-dynamic duo looked at each other uncertainly and then started sluggishly demonstrating seemingly random movements. My fellow student and I awkwardly stood there, uncertain what we were supposed to do.

When it finally dawned on the instructors to—you know—*instruct*, they asked us to imitate their movements. Because they had failed to provide us with any context, these movements felt, well, ridiculous. To the untrained eye, a lot of these basic forms look like the movements of an enthusiastic drunk looking for their dropped keys. Well, at least that's what *I* looked like. It wasn't until the end of class, when the teachers finally played with each other, linking all the movements into a cohesive and beautiful sequence, that the pieces finally, literally, came together. It turned out we had learned a lot in the two hours we were there, but we didn't realize it without putting all the pieces into play—into context.

We've covered a lot of ground so far in this book, and there are a lot of pieces whirling around. You may be feeling a little bit like I did in capoeira class, staring at something you don't quite know what to make of. So I want to make sure that, unlike them, I contextualize how the system and the practice come together.

You may have heard this saying before: "Give a man a fish, and you feed him for a day. Teach a man to fish, and you feed him for a lifetime." In the Bullet Journal method, the system is the rod. The practice provides the line and the lure. They're two separate parts that can only be fully appreciated when you see them come together. A powerful way to experience this, and deepen your understanding, is by learning how to customize and design your own Collections.

Designing your own Collections shows you how to make BuJo your own. In the process, you put into practice all of the elements we've covered in this book so far. It's part organization, part soul-searching, part dream-weaving. These ingredients, when combined mindfully, will allow you to continuously reshape your Bullet Journal into a tool that can help you do far more than just order your chaos. It's here where we can truly leverage the flexibility of this methodology to chart a path toward what shines forth with intention.

One thing that keeps bringing me back to the Bullet Journal—what allows it to remain relevant after all these years—is how it continues to adapt to my changing needs. Your Bullet Journal can become whatever *you* need it to be. Figuring out what you need it to be, how it can best serve you, *is* part of this practice, and it will change over time.

In this part of the book, we'll examine how to go about doing that by working on a project that requires us to consider different kinds of content. It will allow us to explore different ways of using the Bullet Journal to tackle challenges, deconstruct them, and design custom layouts—or templates—that will help us organize a plan of action.

Rather than being prescriptive, these chapters serve to highlight considerations that I hope will prove useful as you set out to make a Bullet Journal of your own.

Caveat

As exciting as it can be to dive into customization, if you're new to Bullet Journaling, I suggest holding off on implementing your own more complex Collections until you're comfortable using what you've learned in Parts II and III. I recommend at least two to three months of basic Bullet Journaling before you start experimenting with your Collections. It's important that you feel comfortable with the day-to-day features of the methodology before you start augmenting it. If you're just getting started, this section is intended to provide a glimpse of how you'll be able to greatly extend the functionality of your Bullet Journals when you're ready.

Every tool and technique that I've introduced so far serves a purpose both on its own and as part of a whole. The Bullet Journal method is a productivity ecosystem of different techniques and philosophies. Each helps the rest flourish. Before you introduce a new species, I urge you to better understand the local population. Once you do, you'll improve your chances of customizing your Bullet Journal practice so that it will bear fruit.

KEY CONCEPTS

Extend your BuJo with Custom Collections

Your Bullet Journal can become anything you
need it to be. Figuring out what you need it to be
is part of the practice. A simple guideline is. . .

Custom Collections should serve a purpose

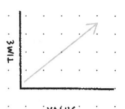

Make sure that the Collections you maintain
are adding value to your life. Productivity is
about carefully investing your time. If you
find yourself struggling. . . .

Define your motivations

Before you figure out how to best do something,
clarify why you're doing it in the first place.

Study your effort

Each Collection is an attempt to learn. It's
important to study your Collections, both the
ones that worked as well as the ones that didn't,
to see what you can take for the next round.

Iterate not only what you're working on,
but how you're working on it!

Less, but better

Function over form

Your notebook does not have to be beautiful to be valuable. Design should always serve a purpose. If it also happens to be beautiful, great! As long as it does not get in the way.

VS

Future-proof your design

Your notebooks tell the story of your life. Make sure your designs make that story easy to follow, both today and years from now.

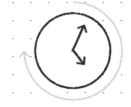

Community

One of the most valuable resources of the Bullet Journal is its community. It's contributed countless examples and applications. If you're stuck, or need inspiration, search your favorite social network for:

#bulletjournal or #bujo

learn to share
share to learn

CUSTOM COLLECTIONS

Content precedes design. Design in the absence of
content is not design, it's decoration.
—JEFFREY ZELDMAN

The Bullet Journal's four core Collections (Index, Future Log, Monthly Log, and Daily Log) will serve you well in most cases. That said, Bullet Journal embraces the fact that one size does not fit all. What if you need to keep track of something in a way that's not presented in this book? This is where Custom Collections come in.

A Custom Collection is designed
to serve a specific need.

It can be as simple as a shopping list or as complicated as a long-term project. Creating Custom Collections is a creative, enjoyable, and rewarding aspect of Bullet Journaling because you're empowering yourself to solve your own challenges!

Whereas the Daily Log is designed as a catchall, Custom Collections should serve a specific purpose. Avoid being an information hoarder! I've been guilty of this myself, creating Collections to track the TV shows I've watched, restaurants I've patronized, and other minutiae. I call these "junk drawer" Collections. There's nothing wrong with tracking what you're doing in a Collection, as long as you plan to do something constructive with the information. An aspiring filmmaker might want to track films she's seen as part of her education: *Am I saturating myself with thrillers and not studying comedy?* Someone who continually falls off the exercise wagon might track workout data and fitness milestones as a way to monitor and encourage continued progress—or spot trends where he falters. (Holidays? Those monthly poker nights? After yet another blind date gone bad?) Junk drawer Collections, in contrast, have limited longevity because they don't provide insight.

If there's nothing to be learned from the information in a Collection, it provides little value, and chances are you'll lack the incentive needed to maintain it. Don't waste your time tending Collections that won't add value to your life.

Three Key Sources for Custom Collections

1. Goals

Goals are important, because they (should) hold the promise of meaning, providing direction and purpose. They also tend to be complex, involving a lot of moving parts. Custom Collections can help us deconstruct a goal into its elements so we can tackle them one at a time.

2. Challenges

Is there some part of your life that's consistently making you feel angry, anxious, overwhelmed, or self-critical? Once you've figured out what the challenge is, creating a Custom Collection tailored to address said challenge can prove very useful. It provides a dedicated space that helps you gather and clarify your thoughts so that you can focus on developing a solution and tracking your progress.

3. Tasks

Many Collections begin their life posing as simple Tasks, like "• Plan vacation!" During the course of your Daily Reflections (page 134), you may identify Tasks harboring a warren of other Tasks. The "Plan vacation" Task, for example, has many moving parts. Left as a singular action item, it will feel overwhelming, which puts it at risk of becoming an object of procrastination and a source of anxiety. Planning a vacation should be a cause for excitement, not angst. So let's choose that for our Custom Collection project.

Quick sidenote, speaking of planning vacations: Studies suggest that looking forward to fun events we planned, like trips, can function as an effective method to elevate our mood and sense of well-being.[56] It's not the trip so much as the anticipation leading up to the trip that can prove both motivational and uplifting. This can be especially helpful when we're working our way through an otherwise challenging time. Through planning, we're setting a course for what shines forth and basking in the glow as we make our way there.

First Steps

To begin this project, let's start by creating our first Collection. So we flip to our next blank spread and add the project Topic: "Hawaii Vacation." That sounds like a lovely alternative to Brooklyn, which as I write this is being blanketed in snow by yet another whopping nor'easter . . . on the first day of spring no less.

Brainstorm

I like to kick off every project in my notebook by using the first pages of my Collection for Brainstorming. These pages are dedicated to capturing initial thoughts, no matter what form they take, be they single words, images, mind maps, etc. This spread is here for you to unload your ideas, get excited, and see what you can shake loose through free association.

But sometimes we're so welded to our day-to-day (both in our doing and in our thinking) that this kind of blue-skying can actually be daunting, making it hard to know where to begin. If that's you, keep reading.

Examine Your Motivations

When creating a Collection for a project—be it writing a book, re-doing the basement, or planning a vacation—a good place to start is by examining our motivation. *Why* are we taking on this project? What need does it address? To have more quality family time? To relax and refresh through surfing and/or forest bathing? Whatever it is, it's okay. We're asking just to get the wheels turning so we can unearth the underlying cause of our motivation.

Why is getting at the underlying cause so important? Motivation doesn't exist in a vacuum. It results from our pain, frustration, or desire. Whatever the case may be, we need to surface it before we can assure that our efforts aren't misdirected. By identifying our true motivations, we increase the potential impact of our actions.

*In other words, understanding **why you feel compelled** to do something will help you better define **how** to do something.*

As noted earlier, our first opportunity to clarify our intention is when we pause to consider a Topic name that captures the essence of what this project is about. Sometimes, though, we need a little more detail than that. In times like these, it can help to write out a brief mission statement to define *why* we're doing something, *what* we hope to get out of the experience, and *how* we will go about doing it. You can even use this script if it's helpful:

I want to _____ [what] so that I can _____ [why] by _____ [how].

So in this case, the mission statement could be:

I want to go on vacation so that I can relax by not being in the office.

Now, while there's nothing wrong with this mission statement, digging a little deeper could help you uncover how this trip could connect with something meaningful to you. After all, you don't need to travel to be out of the office. What is it about *this* trip that really excites you? We can use the Five Whys (page 213) to help us here.

1. Why do you want to go on vacation? To relax.
2. Why? Because work is stressing me out and depressing me.
3. Why? Because it's the same thing day in and day out, and it makes me feel lonely.
4. Why? Because my life is confined to my cubicle and my couch, and I don't get to see the people I care about.
5. Why? Because I don't take time for those things.

We've now identified various pain points that we can begin to tackle. Let's start by highlighting some key themes that have surfaced: confinement, boredom, depression, loneliness, and guilt. These are the likely sources of your motivation. The goal for this vacation would then be to alleviate those pain points by experiencing their opposites: freedom, excitement, joy, connection, and pride. Let's rephrase our mission statement to address these desires:

> I want to go on vacation so that I can remind myself what I'm working for (pride) by spending quality time with people I care about (connection) while we have fun (joy) exploring a tropical place together (freedom and excitement).

This simple exercise not only helped us figure out our priorities for our trip, but also gave us some food for thought that we can address later on, when we're calm and tan. Also, keep in mind that this technique can be applied to any project of your choosing. For example:

> I want to write a book so that I can teach people how to have more agency over their life by sharing the knowledge I've found valuable for living intentionally.

Or:

> I want to go to nursing school so that I can help people by learning how to treat illness and suffering.

Feel free to create your own script. Just make sure it helps you dig into your motivation and expose what's most important to you about your venture. Later, when you're in the thick of the process, your mission statement can help remind you of what your priorities are, functioning as a compass if and when you need it.

Writing down this mission statement is also a great way to "wake the page." That's the term I use to describe the act of marking the page for the first time. It's the moment when thought transcends the distance between our inner and outer world, and we breathe life into our ideas. Beginning can be the hardest part. What better way to wake the page than by stating what you want? Don't overthink it; just write down what you feel. It's not a contract. It's just a benevolent way to nudge yourself over the starting line.

DESIGN

*A designer knows he has achieved perfection
not when there is nothing left to add, but
when there is nothing left to take away.*

—ANTOINE DE SAINT-EXUPÉRY

If you've searched for "bullet journal" or "BuJo" online, you may
have seen the elaborately illustrated interpretations people have
created. They're gorgeous—motivating to some, but intimidating
to many others. People assume they can't Bullet Journal because
they're not artists or because their handwriting is too sloppy. Allow
me to lay those concerns to rest. The only thing that matters in
BuJo is the content, not the presentation. If you can elevate both,
then my hat's off to you. But the only artistic skill required is the
ability to draw straightish lines. If you can manage that, then you'll
be fine. As Bullet Journalist Timothy Collinson says: "I must have
the plainest, most minimal style of Bullet Journaling you could
imagine, as I'm no artist and calligraphy is a dream beyond the
horizon. But I can honestly say it's been life changing."

The goal when designing our Collections is to maximize their
functionality, legibility, and sustainability. In this chapter I want to

delve into each, and share some considerations that may prove help-ful when you set out to design your own.

Functionality

Dieter Rams, the industrial designer behind some of the most iconic radios, shavers, and numerous other household objects (some of which are rumored to have inspired the design of the original iPod), used to say *wenniger aber besser*, which loosely translates into "less, but better." It's one of the guiding principles underlying the Bullet Journal method, and it's reflected in the design. Form should never obscure function. Distill your design down to the essential so that you're only focusing on what is meaningful. If you find beautify-ing your notebook *is* essential to maintaining your motivation and productivity, then have at it. Just remember, collections are tools that are meant to help you progress toward your goals, not stand in their way.

Collections should always favor function over form. It's how well a Collection helps you execute its underlying goal that matters.

This is not only true for the design of the templates, but also for the information they contain, like weight, time, distance, names, events, etc. Habit trackers, for example, are Collections designed to help form new behaviors by tracking progress for things like reading, meditating, exercise, water consumed throughout the day, etc. Because there are so many things we could be doing better, there's a temptation to get a little overenthusiastic at first, taking on way too much at a time. Try to avoid tracking six habits simultaneously. This can quickly become overwhelming, burdensome, and demotivating. It will take a lot of time to maintain, and the probability of failing to form a half dozen new habits at the same time is high. Track only the habits that you feel most strongly about now. Be cool. Be selective. As Herr Rams suggests: Start with less, but do it better. You can always add more later. Keep the content of your Collections focused on your priorities.

Another solid measure of a Collection's functionality is how future-proof it is. A well-designed Collection will remain informative long after it has served its purpose. I've created a lot of Collections that made sense at the time, but looking back on them, I couldn't follow my thinking anymore. A great exercise to ensure the longevity of your layout is to design your templates in a way that a stranger could easily understand what they're looking at. To be clear, I'm not suggesting that you share your journal with someone else! It's just that our future selves may want to repurpose an effective Collection one day, so let's make it as easy as we can for them to remember how and why it worked.

Your Collections should be as helpful to you
in retrospect as they are in real time.

Every new iteration of your templates should undergo some scrutiny. What worked? What didn't? What little thing can I change to make this work better for me? By keeping your templates lean, it becomes easier to identify opportunities for functional improvement. Keep it simple. Keep it focused. Keep it relevant.

Legibility

Our handwriting is a uniquely revealing form of self expression, often reflecting our inner state. It swells with joy and deteriorates with stress, sometimes to a point where it becomes hard to decipher. Perhaps it was never great to begin with. We take it for granted that we're stuck with the cards we're dealt, but even something as ingrained as our handwriting can greatly benefit from a little attention.

If you struggle with legibility, try experimenting with alternate types of lettering and/or writing instruments. You may be surprised at how well your handwriting responds to even the subtlest of changes. For example, I found that writing in all caps with fineliner pens solved two legibility problems: It forced me to be more deliberate in shaping letters and to be more economical with my word choices. Though awkward at first, this intentional change ended up pardoning many a passable idea formerly condemned to my cursive hieroglyphics.

Use this as an excuse to dip your toe into the pen and ink world. It's rich with elegance, heritage, and history, bringing to bear hundreds of years of knowledge of how to lay ink onto paper. From fountain to felt-tip pens, there is a lot to explore. Chances are, you'll find something that will help improve your skill or, at the very least, your appreciation for handwriting. Just be careful not to let your quest for the perfect pen or paper get in the way of your writing. Your pen is not a wand, it's just a tool. It's you who brings the magic to the page.

Legibility is not just about what we put on the page, it's also about what we leave off. Claude Debussy once said that music is the space between notes.[57] In graphic design, that space is imaginatively referred to as "white space." It's not an afterthought, it's a very deliberate element used to increase focus, structure, and clarity. Give your designs room to breathe. In order for your templates to remain legible, they should tend away from density. Play with scale, add more space—or padding—to text, table cells, or list items. Sometimes that means less fits on a page. That's fine. How we frame our information will go a long way toward increasing legibility, comprehension, and our sanity. We only make room for what matters.

Sustainability

Maintaining Collections takes time and energy, so it's important to make sure they're worth the commitment. Every Collection that you've learned about so far was a solution to a specific challenge. The Index (page 99) resulted from the frustration of not being able to locate content in my notebook. The Monthly Log (page 90) came about in response to wanting to have an overview of responsibilities and time. These and the others have proved valuable time and time again, easily earning the attention required to maintain them.

You want to make sure that maintaining a Collection doesn't feel like a chore. Most accounts of people falling off the Bullet Journal wagon turn out to be people who spent too much time decorating their pages. There's nothing wrong with decoration—unless it becomes a drag. That means the balance is off; if you don't feel the reward is worth the effort, simplify.

The good news is that you'll naturally be able to weed out unsustainable Collections during your Monthly or Yearly Migration. If you haven't updated a given Collection, you'll know that it's not adding much value to your life. It's okay to let it go. It's not a failure; it's a valuable lesson that can be applied to future template designs. You need to learn how something doesn't work in order to design something that will. Be sure your frustration or disappointment doesn't rob you of that opportunity.

A key part of Bullet Journaling is learning what you're curious about and what you naturally gravitate toward. Evaluating your Collections during Migration quickly reveals what kinds of things actually hold your attention and what you struggle with. You can learn a lot by how frequently you update a Collection. This is not only true for your actions, but also for the way you organize your thoughts. Over time, you'll figure out what layouts help you think more clearly, be more focused, and allow you to make meaningful progress. Not only are you becoming more intentional about *what* you're doing, but also *how* you're doing it. This is how Bullet Journal helps you learn how to design your own tools for continual improvement.

PLANNING

If you fail to plan, you are planning to fail!
—Benjamin Franklin

You can't plan your way out of failure, but you *can* greatly increase the odds of success by doing a little legwork before you dive into your project. Whether planning a trip to Hawaii, a website relaunch, or a presentation, you'll ensure the best use of your time and resources if you pause to define what the parameters and variables are before figuring out how to structure a plan of action.

Professional cooks have all their ingredients prepped and laid out well before they start to assemble their plates. The vegetables are chopped, garnishes minced, the surfaces are cleaned. This is known as the *mise en place*, or *mise* (rhymes with "cheese"), which is French for "putting in place." This practice allows the cook to focus on what's important: assembling the meal. In your Bullet Journal, you're the chef.

Collections, like meals, are the sum of their parts. In order to design a meaningful Collection, you need to define the "ingredients" you have to work with. Depending on what you're working on, these ingredients take the form of values like sessions, weight, distance, etc. Your Collection will be designed to clearly store and order these values.

Let's map this onto our "Hawaii Vacation" Collection. While we're brainstorming, we'll identify various pieces of information—ingredients, if you will—that need to be sorted and put in place. We do this by asking ourselves small questions, like *Where do I want to go? What do I want to do? When do I want to go? And what's my budget?* We can repurpose these questions to define categories like Destinations, Activities, Time, and Budget. Right after your Brainstorm spread, list these categories out along with their considerations, so you can start to structure the framework for your project (page 252).

Now we have our list of all the things we need to consider. We can create Subcollections in our Bullet Journal to tackle each individually. Let's start with Destinations, because it will require the most research.

Research

Every undertaking is full of unknowns, but doing your homework can go a long way in helping you overcome one of the most challenging phases of any endeavor: getting started. First of all, it eases you into the project by simply becoming more familiar with the landscape. The more aware we are of what to expect, the less we'll end up fumbling about when we get there. This may seem obvious, but a lot of people begin their big project with a dramatic gesture or proclamation with no idea what they're up against. Though the effort

VACATION TO HAWAII

MISSION STATEMENT

"I want to go on vacation so that I can remind myself what I'm working for by spending quality time with people I care about while we have fun exploring a tropical place together."

DESTINATIONS

- Where do I want to go in Hawaii?

ACTIVITIES

- What do I want to do?
- What do my travel companions like to do?

TIME

- Vacation days available
- Flight time
- Local commute time
- Activities duration

BUDGET

- Flight
- Car rental
- Lodging
- Gas
- Food
- Activities

may be commendable, it may also be short-lived, quickly succumbing to entirely avoidable problems.

Let's say you want to become a vegetarian. With a bit of research and planning, you'll know how to stock your fridge and how to prepare, say, a week's worth of tasty meals to get you started. That way you don't hit day one of your new life with an empty fridge, an empty stomach, and an empty plate—unless you count hefty helpings of frustration, discouragement, and overwhelm, which you wash down with a steak burrito of shame. As we've discussed, overwhelm can quickly drain us of our motivation and excitement. We can mitigate this by educating ourselves ahead of time.

On the flip side, be careful not to fall down the research rabbit hole. Educating ourselves can be fun and feel productive, but for some it becomes a way to avoid getting on with the process. The longer you research, the more options you will surface, which can also be overwhelming. We want to avoid "analysis paralysis." We need to research, but we also need to make progress. How do we do both, in the proper proportions? This is where time boxing (page 178) comes into play.

Time boxing will give you both a starting and an end point to your research sessions, providing the structured space needed for exploration. Some people like to set a timer during their research sessions to help them focus and keep from being sucked into the black hole of the internet.

When you're figuring out your research time slot, also limit the number of total sessions you have available. For example, when planning your trip to Hawaii, one of your first Tasks is to research its several islands to determine which you want to travel to. Each island offers *a lot* of different exciting things to explore. To prevent your research from turning into its own form of distraction, allot yourself something like two 30-minute research sessions per island, and block it out on your calendar. If you need more time, that's fine, just quarantine your research so that the sessions remain productive and finite.

The first thing you want to do during your initial research session is to create your "Destinations" Subcollection. On the first page, we'll list out all of the islands we have to choose from for reference. Each following page will focus on one specific island, listing the activities that would warrant a trip to that island. Is it the amazing volcano hikes? The great surfing? The villages where you can meander? For now, don't think of how (*How will I afford it? How would I get there? Where would I stay?*); we'll get to that in a bit. First, focus on finding *what* would best support your mission statement, the reason for this trip.

Just as the moves of the capoeira instructors I mentioned earlier made little sense without context, so, too, will taking action without planning. Without a plan, action tends to result in wasted motion, energy, and time, often culminating in the disappointment of failure. Yes, I realize that our project example is "just" a vacation, but it's our precious investment of time, energy, and hard-earned money. Why not make the most out of it?

LISTS

Since we're working with various types of data in our vacation project (dates, times, dollars, etc.), we can optimize each type of content by tailoring layouts to best support their function. Your budget and your itinerary, for example, serve two very different purposes, so why should they share the same design?

The most basic template is the list. Lists provide an effective, convenient way to organize content and are simple to create. They allow us to capture information quickly by encouraging us to keep our entries short and to the point. Few design conventions can do so much with so little. It's why the list is the core design pattern in the Bullet Journal.

Let's take a look at a list detailing all the fun activities we found researching Mauna Kea, one of the Hawaiian islands (page 256). In an ideal world, we would have time to enjoy everything on our list, but alas, we don't. Lists can quickly become bloated and overwhelming, so in this chapter we explore some quick ways to curate our lists so they remain focused and manageable.

MAUNA KEA

* The Emerald Pools

  The Lava Fields

* Volcanic Forest

  Wild Stingray Beach

* Night Market

  Moonoa Yoga School

  ~~Black Sand Beach~~

  Green Sand Beach

  Turtle Beach

  Volcano Beach

Prioritizing

When we're drafting a list, like the one for our vacation, we're just gathering data: This sounds like fun or that seems important, and so on. We get caught up in the capture, which is fine as long as the list serves a purpose. Once our list is more or less complete, it's time to take a step back and reflect on it. Which items excite you? Which don't? Weigh each entry on a mental scale and take a first pass using the "*" Signifier to prioritize the items you feel strongest about or are the most time sensitive, and strike off the items you feel "meh" about. We're not here to design a lukewarm life.

Lastly, there's often a human element that we need to consider while we prioritize. In this case, if you're traveling with others, then a good place to start culling your list is by considering your companions' allergies, likes, dislikes, etc. It's not necessarily about sacrificing what you want to do, but it can quickly tip the scales for options that you're hung up on: black or green sand beach? Everyone else has seen black? Green it is!

Context

In the previous example, you'll see the list of all the exciting things that seem fun to do on Mauna Kea, our hypothetical Hawaiian vacation. That's a good start, but this list doesn't really provide a lot of context. It's like being at a restaurant where everything on the menu looks great. It's not until we see the prices, ingredients, and calorie counts that we quickly narrow down our options. Context provides information that will help us prioritize. To that end, let's add some parameters to our list that will help facilitate our decision-making by adding some context: location, time, and cost.

I added the time "T" column so that I don't show up somewhere just to realize it's closed on Wednesdays because Big Sammy, the owner, in his infinite rational wisdom, decided *Wednesdays are not for working.* It's happened. Noting opening and closing times also provides context as you schedule your days.

I've denoted location (in the "L" column) by "N" for north, "S" for south, "E" for east, "W" for west, and "C" for central. This helps me understand roughly where my points of interest are in relationship to one another so I can make better decisions about efficient commuting and lodging. (I don't know about you, but I'd rather spend more time being places than getting there.) Noting the locations also provides a nice menu of nearby fallback options should a given activity not pan out.

The cost "$" column is pretty self-explanatory. Including prices serves as a data point we can later use to edit down our list once we've determined our budget. To be clear, just because something is expensive does not mean it needs to be taken off our list. It's simply information we can later use to help facilitate our choices.

Mauna Kea	T	L	$
* The Emerald Pools	W / 9-4	N	124
The Lava Fields	W / 11-6	S	65
* Volcanic Forest	Mult	W	32
Wild Stingray Beach		NE	10/hr
Turtle Beach	M-T / 8-4	W	
* Night Market		SW	
Moonoa Yoga School		W	
~~Black Sand Beach~~		E	
Green Sand Beach		NW	
Surfboard rental		W	
Surfboard rental 2		W	

Invariably a lot of options on our list will remain for now because they all seem fun. That's okay. As we progress through our planning, we'll revisit our list and filter the items through new considerations surfaced by the other Collections we'll set up later. As with all the core Collections, your Custom Collections can influence each other. To better understand this, we'll create Collections for both our itinerary and our budget.

SCHEDULES

Time is a critical consideration for any project, even (especially!) travel. So with our list of activities in place, the next step is to contextualize them in terms of time. For that we will need a Collection designed for that purpose, like an itinerary. Chances are you've created an itinerary before. If so, revisit your old friend and reminisce. Study it and reflect on how both the design and the experience it stored suited you.

What did you learn? Do you tend to be overoptimistic and overpack your days? Did that leave you feeling stressed and/or exhausted? Or did you wing it a little too much, only to discover that there were museum shows you didn't know about and allow time for, restaurants where the maître d' coolly informed you that the tables book up weeks in advance, and sweet little day trips that weren't even on your radar? This is not about dwelling on the past; it's about reapplying what you learned to improve your odds of having a better experience. What would you do differently this time around?

Let's start by figuring out when to go. There's rarely a perfect time for anything, but don't let that be your excuse. Be practical about it. You'll want to get the most amount of time possible. If you're a nine-to-five worker, the best way to hack your travel may be to lump it in with national holidays, thereby extending your time off without sacrificing too many paid vacation days.

Once we know our travel dates, we can start to design our schedule template accordingly. This is one of the few instances where I'll use both a pen and a pencil to design a Collection. There are a lot of decisions that need to be made here, and chances are you'll have to keep updating things as you go. Always factor usage into your design. If you're working on a Collection that is designed to order sequences such as events or activities, make sure to use tools that will allow for the necessary flexibility.

1. To set up my template, I considered the relevant variables: where, when, and what (page 263). The first column addresses the where. Since we'll be island-hopping, it's rather important to know where we are on which day. In this example, the first column denotes location with the airport code and the page number of that location's Subcollection. I've threaded that destination (page 104) in the Subcollection in case something doesn't work out, so I can quickly pick an alternative from the list. The text is oriented vertically to add some visual friction, making it easier to see once we add the dates. You'll also note that the location column breaks the barrier between days. This helps underscore transition between locations so travel days are easily discernible. Additionally, the location column extends into the following day to different depths. The depth of the bar roughly indicates what time of day the flight is.

2. The next column lists the "when" by running the trip dates down the left margin in chronological order. For added legibility, the dates and the day of the week are given more space so they're easier to see at a glance.

HAWAII ITINERARY

<table>
<tr><td rowspan="4">HNL / 11</td><td>25
TU</td><td>9:00

3:00
7:30</td><td>Check in @ Reef Hotel
Town and beach
Kundalini class
Dinner @ The Rum Barrel</td></tr>
<tr><td>26
WE</td><td>11:30
4:00
5:30
8-10</td><td>Check out
Flight to Mauna Kea
Capoeira class
Manta diving</td></tr>
<tr><td>27
TH</td><td>
3:00
7:30</td><td>Emerald Beach day!
Surf class
Dinner @ The Secret Garden</td></tr>
<tr><td>28
FR</td><td>9:00

3:00
7:30</td><td>Yoga class
Lava fields
Dinner @ Surf House
Night Market</td></tr>
</table>

| MWE / 12 | 29
SA | 9:00
11:00
7:30 | Check out
Flight to HNL
Dinner @ Sushi Kona |

| HNL / 11 | 30
SU | 9:00
11:00
3:00 | Check out
Flight to HO
Dinner @ Jimmies |

1.   2.   3.

3. With dates and locations all figured out, now all that's left to do is plug in our activities. Items toward the top of a cell are scheduled in the morning, with each successive item happening later in the day. Since some activities required booking ahead of time, the activities are preceded by a time. It helps us slot in the remaining activities from our "Destinations" Subcollection accordingly.

You may think this is all very elaborate. Perhaps your travel planning is of the "throw a dart at a map" variety. Again, this is only a fast example to illustrate the considerations that go into crafting and relating your own Collections, no matter what their application may be. This is your journey, but sometimes it's helpful to see how to draw a map before you draft your own.

TRACKERS

You can't manage what you can't measure.
—PETER DRUCKER

A very common type of Custom Collection in Bullet Journals are trackers. These can take pretty much any form you can imagine. I've seen illustrated bookcases lined with the books read by the Bullet Journalist, or pieces of popcorn tracking all the movies someone's watched. Though these clever trackers inject Collections with personality and whimsy, the underlying focus for most successful trackers is to monitor progress toward an intended goal.

Trackers are a great example of how we can take larger goals and deconstruct them into smaller actionable steps. They make potentially intimidating endeavors more manageable, and they keep us honest. Our memories and realities often are not the best of friends. Having a place where you log and objectively monitor your progress can go a long way to keeping you on track.

In our case we'll create a simple budget tracker that will serve two purposes. First, it will allow us to group our priorities on one page so we can see how much the trip will cost us. Second, we can visually monitor our progress toward affording those activities.

I've provided a basic example here for our budget tracker. It's divided into three main columns. The first lists activities. The second focuses on cost by providing an activity's total cost and how much we need to set aside each month. The third is the actual tracker column. Here the costs are spread out across the months leading up to the trip. This way I can quickly see how much I need to save every month, as well as monitor my progress toward my goals. If I happen to miss a month, I can mark that amount in the corresponding cell where I fell short. This allows us to quickly total the balance if necessary.

At the bottom of the tracker you'll note that there is a total. Next to it, you'll see that I've added the months again. This makes it easier for my eye to track the column. Here you will see a "+" for when I add funds above the required minimum and a "–" for how much I fell short.

This layout provides a lot of oversight into the trip's financials. It does so by making room for error. Things come up, and you may not have the cash one month. That's really important to know. When you keep it all in your head it's easy to lose an overview of your progress—or your lack thereof. By keeping a tracker, you'll have a clear picture of where you actually are in the context of where you want to be.

Using Collections to Form Context

Dedicated trackers can be used in conjunction with your Daily Logs to surface even more context. One allows you to measure, while the other can provide some much-needed insight. Did I not

HAWAII BUDGET

EXPENSE	Total / M	4	5	6	7	8	9	10	11
Tickets to Hawaii	1200/150	x	x	x	x	x	x	50	x
Tickets to Mauna Kea	120/15	15	x	x	x	x	x	x	x
Ticket to Honolulu	140/17	x	18	x	x	x	x	x	x
Honolulu Hotel	360/45	x	x	x	x	x	x	x	x
Mauna Kea Hotel	235/29	30	x	x	x	x	x	x	x
Surfing Lessons	100/13	x	x	x	x	x	x	x	x
Lava Fields	25/3	x	x	x	x	x	x	x	x
Diving With Mantas	100/13	x	x	45	x	x	x	x	x
Food Budget	350/44	x	44	x	x	x	x	x	x
Gas	100/13	x	x	x	x	x	x	x	x
Misc	500/62	x	x	x	x	65	x	x	x
TOTAL	3,230/404	4	5	6	7	8	9	10	11
	+					217		50	
	−	45	62	45	0	65	0	50	0

go to the gym because I was lazy, sick, or sad? What were the circumstances that did or did not allow me to make progress?

Though making progress is clearly desirable, it shouldn't be your sole focus. Only focusing on the outcome will often blind you to valuable information that surfaces during the process itself. I would argue that the point of tracking is just as much about cultivating self-awareness as it is about making progress.

In order to make any true progress, you need to understand the effects of your efforts. You need to understand not only *what* is or is not working, but also *why*. Losing 10 pounds is great, but knowing that it had nothing to do with the gym and everything to do with your diet is much more valuable. Now the correlation may not always be that direct, but as long as we are tracking, we are bound to find patterns. That's what's important: becoming aware of cause and effect. The more we know, the more effective we can be, and the more progress we can make.

CUSTOMIZATION

While Custom Collections serve an important purpose in helping your Bullet Journal reflect you in all your infinite variety, it's important to remember we don't always have to reinvent the wheel for every new venture. Often, core Collections can be customized to adapt to our current situation.

When you're at home, for example, chances are your Daily Log will be in work mode, primarily focused on capturing Tasks and organizing your responsibilities. When you travel, however, you go into vacation mode and won't be using your Daily Logs in this task-oriented way—at least you shouldn't be; you're on vacation! Traveling breaks our routine and exposes us to new things. All sorts of thoughts can bubble up that are hard to wrap our head or heart around. One way to take the heat or chill out of a thought is to get it out of your head by writing about it.

Long-Form Journaling

The benefits of long-form journaling are well documented, especially when it comes to stress reduction and combating anxiety. If you're reading this book, you've likely dabbled in some form of more traditional journaling, be it expressive writing or morning pages, at some point in your life. Perhaps you're still actively engaged in the process. I'm often asked how it fits in with the Bullet Journal method, so let's take a look at how we can customize our Daily Log to both capture thoughts quickly *and* facilitate long-form journaling.

When you check in with your Bullet Journal during your Daily Reflection at your hotel or when lying on the beach, jot down any big, interesting, or heavy thoughts as you would any other Note. But it's not just any Note, is it? It's distracting and won't let you go. It warrants more time and attention and needs to be unpacked and examined. When this is the case, all you need to do is turn the Note dash "–" into a plus "+". Now you can quickly scan your Notes and locate the specific thought when you're ready to hunker down to write about it. When you do, take as much room as you need to think. That's what your Bullet Journal is there for, after all. There is no pressure to make this a regular part of your practice. Just know that this helpful tool can be available to you if and when you need it.

12.20.MO

- ○ Went to the green sand beach
- − Fighter jets in the sky.
- ○ Yoga class
  - − Totally out of shape
  - − Felt really stressed
- + Linda needs to give herself more credit
- • Make reservations at the Lazlo
- • Buy more suntan lotion

Linda

I've noticed that lately Linda has become a lot harder on herself than usual, even though things are looking up on her end. The promotion, the new partner, etc. She seems more driven than she ever has. Is it because she is trying to earn her luck? Is this some kind of manifestation of impostor syndrome? Whatever it is, I worry that she will burn herself out. Just worried that not everything is, in fact, as good as she lets on. Where she once went out of her way to "enjoy the moment," she now keeps pushing forward without really acknowledging how much better she is now than a year ago . . .

12.21.TU

- ○ Saw dolphins
- − Totally sunburnt
- • Find time to talk to Linda
- • Call about night market bus

Feel free to create a task based on your long-form entry

Habit Tracking

Another example of customizing an existing Collection is by integrating a habit tracker into your Monthly Log. This simple addition makes it easy to monitor habits you're trying to add or subtract. Let's say I want to track how many times I cook, read, and go to the gym in a month. Under the dates, I'll add a small key (page 273): C = Cook, R = Read, G = Gym (this is so my future self will know what I was keeping track of when looking back through this notebook). On the right margin of the page, I'll create three columns: C, R, G. Keep in mind that these columns align with the days of the month, so I can piggyback on the existing template. Then I'll add Task bullets in the cells so I can "X" them off when I successfully take action. This tracker makes it very easy to see how diligent I've been. Again, it's a subtle addition, but it adds a lot of functionality.

Some people add the weather to their Daily Log; other people add affirmations. Feel free to adjust everything I've shown you. As always, do what works for you.

To be clear, I'm not saying *do whatever you want*! Be sure that any additions or customizations prove themselves helpful over and over again. Less, but better.

January

			C	R	G
1	M	Dinner with Mark	X	X	X
2	T		X	X	X
3	W	Drinks with Sam	X	X	X
4	T	Handed in Might Co. presentation	X	X	•
5	F		•	X	•
6	S		•	X	X
7	S	Sokura convention	X	X	X
8	M		X	•	X
9	T	Lisa's birthday	X	X	X
10	W		X	X	X
11	T	Intro to Krav	•	X	•
12	F		•	X	•
13	S	Drinks with team	X	X	X
14	S		X	X	X
15	M		•	X	X
16	T	A.I. lecture	X	X	X
17	W	Spin class	X	X	X
18	T		X	X	•
19	F	Ramen with Darby @ Ichiran	X	X	•
20	S	Movie with Niclas	X	•	X
21	S		X	X	X
22	M		•	X	•
23	T	Tim's birthday	•	X	X
24	W		X	X	X
25	T	Won Victor account!!	X	•	•
26	F		X	X	•

C	Cooking
R	Reading
G	Gym

Remember to add a key or you might forget what you were tracking later

COMMUNITY

There is no better way to exemplify the potential applications of the Bullet Journal methodology than by shining a spotlight on its community. It spans nearly every race, creed, continent, and industry. This diversity is reflected in the countless solutions the community has created to tackle the common and not so common challenges we face in our limited time here.

You may have noticed that some chapters in Part II contain #hashtags under the titles. These hashtags will help you search social networks like Instagram and Pinterest for community examples, for inspiration, and for support. Here are a few more: #bulletjournalkey, #bulletjournalgratitudelog, #bulletjournalfoodlog, #bulletjournal moodlog, #bulletjournalgymlog.

If you find that a little overwhelming, start by visiting bullet journal.com. There you'll find curated tutorials, examples, and lists of additional resources, largely contributed by the community. In the meantime, I've included some clever and inventive examples in the pages that follow.

Before you turn the page, though, please keep in mind that what you're about to see comes from years of exploration and practice.

Each Bullet Journal is a journey into the self. These Bullet Journalists have submitted the following examples from their Journals to share the impact that Bullet Journal has had on their lives, in hopes of inspiring you to pursue your journey in your own inimitable way.

Kim Alvarez (@tinyrayofsunshine)

In August 2013, I was looking around online for techniques and ideas to help me organize my life. I happened upon an article on Lifehacker about the Bullet Journal, and I was mesmerized as I watched Ryder's tutorial video. "What a genius system!" I exclaimed as I eagerly reached over to grab a half-used notebook to give it a fresh life.

About 20 minutes later, my boyfriend arrived and I enthusiastically showed him the video, and we were so blown away at its simplicity that we both started Bullet Journaling right then and there.

I've always loved notebooks and spending time journaling, drawing, planning, and writing down my memories, so the Bullet Journal is a wonderful solution to encompass my medley of interests.

One of the ideas I was really excited to incorporate into my Bullet Journal was the practice of Gratitude Logging. I always loved thinking about and writing down what I was thankful for ever since I discovered that it was a practice that could instantly make me feel better by challenging me to notice the tiny sunny moments in everyday life. I appreciate that I can capture those meaningful moments as needed.

The flexibility of the system is incredibly welcoming, refreshing, and empowering. Each day I can start where I am and create exactly what I need.

I'm deeply grateful to Ryder for kindly sharing this life-changing system with the world and creating a movement toward simplicity, mindfulness, and intentionality with a unique analog method!

Gratitude Log

I'M GRATEFUL THAT RYDER SHARED THE BULLET JOURNAL WITH THE WORLD!

I'M GRATEFUL TO LIVE IN A SAFE, PEACEFUL, & LOVING HOME

I'M GRATEFUL TO HAVE A COZY READING CHAIR TO ENJOY READING ON

I'M GRATEFUL FOR RAINBOWS THAT VISIT ME

I'M GRATEFUL FOR MY MIND & HEART

I'M GRATEFUL FOR THE KINDNESS OF OTHERS

I'M GRATEFUL FOR REFRESHING SHOWERS

I'M GRATEFUL FOR SUNNY DAYS

I'M GRATEFUL FOR THE LOVELY FRIENDS I'VE MADE IN MY LIFE

I'M GRATEFUL FOR ALL THE EXPERIENCES THAT LED TO THIS MOMENT

I'M GRATEFUL FOR RANDOM FRIENDLY INTERACTIONS WITH OTHERS

I'M GRATEFUL FOR SPECIAL SNAILMAIL

I'M GRATEFUL THAT MY THOUGHTS & IDEAS RESONATE WITH OTHERS

Kara Benz (@boho.berry)

My Bullet Journal journey began in August of 2015.

After 15 years in the restaurant industry, I had just opened a handmade jewelry shop on Etsy. In an effort to get myself organized, I'd been hopping around from planner to planner, trying out all of the preprinted layouts. Nothing seemed to work for me. I even tried some digital apps, but still, nothing offered the flexibility that I needed for my busy life and growing business.

The idea struck me that I needed to create my own planner, but I had no idea where to start. While searching for "DIY Planner" on Pinterest, I stumbled across the concept of Bullet Journaling.

There was not a lot of BuJo inspiration out there at the time, but after reading through the Bullet Journal website and adapting other ideas that I'd seen, I started my very first BuJo.

It's now two and a half years later, and I don't think I ever could have imagined how much this simple system would change my life.

I'm a part of a community of people who "get" me, and I've discovered a lot about myself in the process. I've gotten my life organized. I've grown so much. And I've had the opportunity to inspire others along the way.

Some of my favorite Collections are my weekly/daily hybrid layouts. On Sundays, I sit down and lay out my week, including important events and appointments. Throughout the week, I add in my daily tasks, take notes, and journal in the leftover space. It's a great way to see my week as a whole on Monday as well as plan the minute details on a daily basis.

DO MORE
*of what makes
you happy*

FEBRUARY

M	T	W	T	F	S	S
			1	2	3	4
5	6	7	8	9	10	11
12	13	14	15	16	17	18
19	20	21	22	23	24	25
26	27	28				

---

mon ● 19

☼ 12 1 2 3 4 5 6 7 8 9 10 11
☾ 12 1 2 3 4 5 6 7 8 9 10 11

**PRESIDENT'S
day.**

⏲ 6AM - OLYMPICS RIDE
→ FILM FP VIDEO
X INBOX ZERO
X NEW STICKER DESIGNS

I feel like I got a lot
accomplished today!
Ready to take
on the weekend!

52°
49°

---

tue 20

☼ 12 1 2 3 4 5 6 7 8 9 10 11
☾ 12 1 2 3 4 5 6 7 8 9 10 11

Amanda B'DAY!

→ RESHOOT
→ CLEAN/ORGANIZE OFFICE
X RESEARCH FLYLADY

I was so exhausted
all day today. Did a
lot of work on my
laptop but the day
definitely
didn't go as
planned.

71°
55°

---

wed 21

☼ 12 1 2 3 4 5 6 7 8 9 10 11
☾ 12 1 2 3 4 5 6 7 8 9 10 11

X PREP FILES FOR MANUF.
→ SCHEDULE APPT W/ ACCT.
X REPLY TO EMAILS
X GO OVER PLANNERCON
  WORKSHOP STUFF

Still felt super tired
all day. Good call on
performing the videos!
Made some great progr-
ess on my
CH on my
font though!

77°
45°

---

thu 22

☼ 12 1 2 3 4 5 6 7 8 9 10 11
☾ 12 1 2 3 4 5 6 7 8 9 10 11

⏲ 2:30P - CRATEJOY CALL
→ FILM PLAN WITH ME
→ RESHOOT FP VIDEO
X SCHED. APPT. W/ ACCOUNTANT
X FINISH FONT

Felt exhausted again
all day. Turns out the
"Milena Crash" is a thing
and I was right about
it all being
hormonal.

45°
30°

---

fri ◑ 23

☼ 12 1 2 3 4 5 6 7 8 9 10 11
☾ 12 1 2 3 4 5 6 7 8 9 10 11

⏲ 8AM - FT @ PH RACE
⏲ 10:30AM - MYCHA VET
~~- NEWSLETTER~~
X PAYROLL
X FILM PLAN WITH ME
X WORK ON FONT
→ RESHOOT FP VIDEO

another low energy
day but I still managed
to get quite a
lot done!

45°
43°

---

sat 24

☼ 12 1 2 3 4 5 6 7 8 9 10 11
☾ 12 1 2 3 4 5 6 7 8 9 10 11

⏲ 12:45P - PZE RIDE
X CLEAN/ORGANIZE OFFICE
X PUBLISH PWM

Still felt pretty tired
but I was able to get
everything done and
still have plenty of
time to sub. overall
a pretty good day!

49°
45°

---

sun 25

☼ 12 1 2 3 4 5 6 7 8 9 10 11
☾ 12 1 2 3 4 5 6 7 8 9 10 11

→ MEAL PLAN
→ COMMISSARY

had a pretty great
day today. caught
up on some shows
and also wrote a
bunch of letters for
incoming.

54°
41°

Dee Martinez (@decadethirty)

It was the end of August 2012, surrounded by a sporadic celestial formation of neuroanatomy textbooks with their pages marked by scraps of paper scrawled with reminders (most notably to "get some sleep"), and clinical notes and lecture slides with their haphazard array of highlighted prose, that I realized my organization and planning system needed a change. After almost ten years of "fitting into" traditional planners, Ryder's intuitive system came at the right time, and bolstered how I planned and achieved my tasks.

Since then, the Bullet Journal has seen me through numerous life milestones—finishing my postgraduate studies, moving interstate for a new career, my wedding, opening a small sideline online business, buying and moving into a new house, pregnancy and baby planning, and my new life as a working parent. You name it, the Bullet Journal has helped me plan with intention, manage my time more effectively, accomplish some of my life goals, and tackle my daily tasks with less anxiety. It has also allowed me to become a part of and contribute to a burgeoning online community of planners.

I plan in a minimalist style—no fancy date headers, flourishes, colors, or stickers—but surprisingly, the Collection that has had the greatest impact is my hand-lettered memories. The format has changed over the years, but the purpose has remained the same—a memory from the day written in creative text. The process allows me to integrate memory keeping with my lifelong obsession with hand lettering, and facilitates in helping me take a mindful pause in my day.

Eddy Hope (@itseddyhope)

Hey, I'm Eddy. A self-employed family man working in the social media industry. Managing multiple client accounts and strategies can be tough, so I sought out ways to help me stay organized. There was much talk about digital tools, but I found that searching for the perfect digital productivity setup is like trying to swim through coal. Until I came across the Bullet Journal during 2013. Touting itself as a rapid logging method for completing and tracking tasks and projects using nothing more than a notebook and a pen. I began to rely on it for anything important, plus . . . what's cooler than carrying around a notebook?

After many months of successful use I developed a need for a way to schedule future events. I tried finding an existing method or "hack" that solved this issue. I found nothing of use but noticed I wasn't the only one feeling the same way. So I decided to create my own system. "The Calendex" was born. A calendar/index hybrid that merges the visual representation of a calendar with the function of an Index. A neat table layout provides a handy bird's-eye view of all upcoming events, meetings, deadlines, etc., so you can see immediately if you are free or otherwise engaged.

I'm proud to say that The Calendex (thecalendex.com) is now a popular, fully fledged, stand-alone analog method for planning or scheduling future events that boasts a growing community of passionate fans from around the globe.

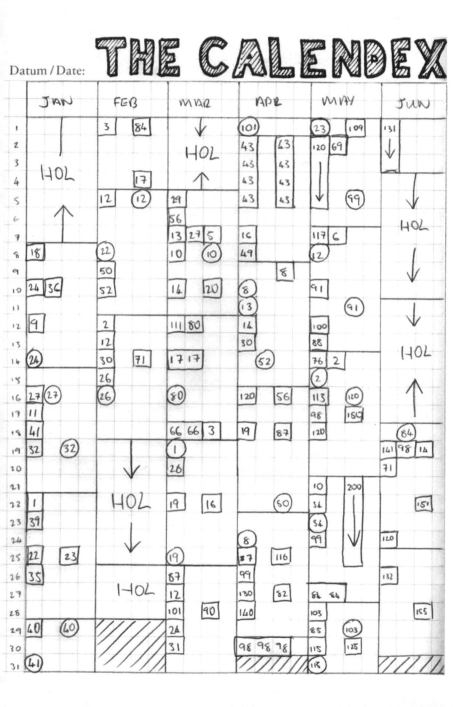

V

THE END

• • •

THE CORRECT WAY TO BULLET JOURNAL

One of the things I love most about watching the Bullet Journal method evolve in the world is how diverse and inventive the interpretations are. I choose to keep my Bullet Journal very minimal. Others choose to make their journals significantly more exciting to look at. It may appear as though no two Bullet Journals are the same. I suppose this is why I'm often asked if there's a correct way to Bullet Journal. It begs a different, more fundamental question: Is there a wrong way to Bullet Journal? The short answer is yes.

I think that part of the Bullet Journal's success stems from its ability to become different tools to different people. Though I strongly advise starting out simple, if spending the time to embellish your Bullet Journal motivates you, makes you more productive, and brings you joy, then you're doing it right. If you look forward to coming back to your journal and feel that it's your ally, then you're doing it right.

It's not about how your journal looks; it's about how it makes you feel and how effective it is.

Don't be intimidated by what you see out there. Ultimately, the only standard you should be aspiring to is your own. This is your journey. I don't use that term lightly. Bullet Journaling is a vehicle for self-exploration, to help you discover what *you* care about and the life *you* want to live. Focus on evolving your Bullet Journal to fit your needs. The longer you use it, the more helpful it should become. If that's not the case, then it's time to ask yourself *why*. Is it taking too much time? Are you neglecting your needs by trying to impress others? Are you not making progress? Define the challenge, and ask yourself: *What could I do to make this more helpful to me?*

If you don't know what to do, you'll have one of the most supportive and creative communities in the world as a resource. Chances are there are Bullet Journalists out there who have tackled similar challenges and who are more than happy to share their insights. Whatever challenges you may be facing, know that you're not alone.

PARTING WORDS

My favorite part of *The Wizard of Oz* is when the fellowship discovers that the mighty wizard is nothing more than an aging man, pulling levers behind a curtain. Once he's revealed, Dorothy exclaims, "Oh, you're a very bad man." To which the wizard replies, "Oh, no, my dear, I . . . I'm a very good man—I'm just a very bad wizard."

The fellowship came asking for things they felt they didn't possess: courage, a heart, a brain. They assumed that only the magic of a powerful wizard would be able to grant them things otherwise entirely out of their reach. Though he was indeed a "very bad wizard," for he had no supernatural powers, the *Man* of Oz did possess a skill. He acted as a mirror to those in need, reflecting an image unclouded by doubt and pain. Through simple observation, the Man of Oz helped the fellowship realize that what they desired was within them all along.

The wizard symbolizes our misguided notion that the "cure" to whatever ails us, the missing piece, exists outside of us. We live in a commoditized culture that convinces us that our solutions must be acquired; that *something* or *someone* will finally make us whole. Our search takes us ever farther away from ourselves. Though we can greatly benefit by keeping our minds and hearts open, ultimately we remain our own responsibility.

The Man of Oz could see beyond the surface of things and connect the dots through careful observation, introspection, and a healthy dose of empathy. This is what the Bullet Journal method helps us cultivate within ourselves. It's in no way magical, but it can be a compelling mirror in which we can begin to see ourselves more clearly with each passing day. It can grant us the insight to see just how much power we already possess.

The Bullet Journal method helps facilitate your journey of self-discovery, to realize the agency you can have over your life. It all depends on your willingness to look past your limitations so that you may witness your potential. It's a process of reclaiming responsibility for your experience by finding the courage to look within. There, in the chaos of it all, you'll find, among the countless stars, those that shine forth the brightest. As you chart your course through the ever-unknown waters of tomorrow, you can take comfort in the certainty of knowing that, sink or swim, you dared.

FREQUENTLY ASKED
QUESTIONS

Q: I'm not artistic. Can I still Bullet Journal?

A: Yes. The only thing that matters in BuJo is the content, not the presentation.

Q: When should I start?

A: The best time to begin is always now. That said, an ideal time to start is on the first of the month when you set up your Monthly Log (page 90).

Q: How long should I try it for?

A: If you're new to Bullet Journaling, your first Monthly Migration (page 108) can be a real lightbulb moment. This is where it all begins to click. That's why I highly encourage new Bullet Journalists to stick with it for at least two to three months when testing it out.

Q: What notebook should I use?

A: A high-quality notebook that will last. The two main things to keep in mind are size and quality. If it's too big, you'll never take it with you. If it's too small, it will be impractical. Be sure to get something that's rugged enough to keep up with you, and that can stand the test of time. If you're so inclined, you can purchase the custom Bullet Journal notebook I designed on Bulletjournal.com. It features numbered pages, an Index, a Bullet key, three bookmarks, and more.

Q: Pen vs. pencil?

A: Use what makes your handwriting most legible and doesn't fade. One of the great benefits of Bullet Journaling is that, over time, you assemble a library of notebooks. This library is a wonderful thing to revisit years later.

Q: What if I lose my notebook?

A: Even though a Bullet Journal can be intensely personal, I highly recommend adding a very visible note in the front of the book for people to contact you should you lose it. Leaving your first name and your phone number only should do the trick. Cash rewards are a great incentive, but so are personalized messages. My Bullet Journal fell out of my bag on a train to New York during rush hour, and it was returned to me.

Q: How do I deal with Recurring Tasks?

A: You can create custom bullets (page 80) and add them to your Monthly Logs Calendar page (page 91). This allows you to quickly scan your month and see when that Task or Event is happening.

Q: What do I do about forgetting to check in with my journal?

A: We created an app for that. It's called The Bullet Journal Companion. It's not a BuJo app, but it's a companion app *for* your notebook. It allows you to store your thoughts while you're away from your journal, set reminders to check in, take pictures of your pages, and more. Yes, it's available for iOS and Android.

Q: Is there an app for that?

A: See previous answer and bulletjournal.com/app.

Q: How much space should the Daily Log take up?

A: As much or as little as you need. Life is unpredictable, and that's why the BuJo is designed to evolve organically. Pick up wherever you left off, and avoid hoarding pages.

Q: How do I migrate notebooks?

A: Review your notebook for things that helped you make progress. Only move the things that added value to your life into your next notebook. You can also thread content that you don't want to rewrite (page 104).

Q: What is the difference between a scheduled and a migrated Task?

A: A scheduled Task is a future Task that falls outside the current month, and has been moved backward into the Future Log. A Migrated Task is a current Task that has been moved forward into the Monthly Log (page 90) or a Custom Collection (page 237).

Q: When should I move things from the Future Log?

A: When you're setting up the new Monthly Log (page 90).

Q: How many notebooks should I use a year?

A: As many as you need. I use three to four a year.

Q: How do I use a digital calendar with the Bullet Journal?

A: You can use a digital calendar to replace your Future Log. During the day, capture any dates in your Daily Log, and then when you get a moment, like during Daily Reflection, add them to your calendar.

Q: How long should I take for Daily Reflection?

A: As long as you need. The trick is to be consistent. If you find yourself not doing it, then reduce the amount of time you're spending.

Q: How do you plan and manage multiple projects?

A: When I have multiple projects, I separate them into different Collections, and then I use my Index to quickly access projects later. You can also create a "Dedicated Index" for each project; this is especially useful if the project is big and involved. If you're in school, for example, you can use one Index page per class (page 102).

Q: What do I do with a Task that needs to be completed on a certain day and that day hasn't arrived yet?

A: If it's within the current month, your Daily Reflection will keep you aware of the task. If it's not, you can add it to your Future Log (page 95).

Q: Why do you keep only one item for each day in your Monthly Log? Is this intentional?

A: When I make Bullet Journal tutorials, I only show one item under each day so that it's more legible to my viewers. In my personal Bullet Journal, I Rapid Log two or three items each day. For me, the Monthly Log is about having a bird's-eye view about what I've already done, so I often end up writing down items after they've already happened.

Q: What is the difference between the Task page on the Monthly Log and the Daily Log in general?

A: The purpose of the Daily Log (page 86) is to declutter your mind—you're not really thinking so much about what you're writing down. You just want to get it down on paper. The Tasks that go into the Monthly Log are the ones that you've taken time to consider; you know that they're important and that they're a priority.

Q: How do I reference material from within my Bullet Journal?

A: For that you set up an Index (page 99) and pair it with a technique called Threading (page 104).

Q: How do I reference material from a previous notebook, Bullet Journal or otherwise?

A: By notebook Threading (page 104) or by using the Bullet Journal Companion app. It was designed to extend the functionality of your notebook. You can add your previous notebooks to the app using the "Library" function by uploading pictures of the Index pages and tagging previous notebooks.

I WOULD LIKE TO THANK:

John Maas and Celeste Fine, my agents with Sterling Lord Literistic, for their unwavering guidance, support, and patience.

Leah Trouwborst and Toni Sciarra Poynter, my editors, for their herculean efforts, wisdom, and ability to help me get through to the other side.

The Portfolio team at Penguin Random House for believing in this project and helping bring it together, and to Helen Healey for keeping the Christmas lights untangled.

My readers: Keith Gould, Linda Hoecker, Kim Alvarez, Niclas Bahn, Lisse Grullesman, Rachel Beider, Leigh Ollman, and my folks for their insights that helped me see the forest through the trees.

All the Bullet Journalists who contributed their art, stories, and ideas throughout this book: Dee Martinez, Eddie Hope, Kim Alvarez, Kara Benz, Heather Caliri, Amy Haines, Anthony Gorrity, Rachael M., Timothy Collinson, Cheryl Bridges, Hubert Webb, Bridget Bradley, Olov Wimark, Sandra-Olivia Mendel, Carey Barnett, and Michael S.

The BuJo community for helping spread Bullet Journal around the world. I would not be here without you.

NOTES

1 Neil Irwin, "Why Is Productivity So Weak? Three Theories," *New York Times*, April 28, 2016, https://www.nytimes.com/2016/04/29/upshot/why-is-productivity -so-weak-three-theories.html.

2 Bureau of Labor Statistics, https://www.bls.gov/opub/btn/volume-6/below -trend-the-us-productivity-slowdown-since-the-great-recession.htm.

3 Daniel J. Levitin, "Why the Modern World Is Bad for Your Brain," *The Guardian*, January 15, 2018, https://www.theguardian.com/science/2015/jan /18/modern-world-bad-for-brain-daniel-j-levitin-organized-mind-information -overload.

4 Maria Konnikova, "What's Lost as Handwriting Fades," *New York Times*, June 2, 2014, https://www.nytimes.com/2014/06/03/science/whats-lost-as-handwriting -fades.html.

5 Joan Didion, "On Keeping a Notebook," in *Slouching Towards Bethlehem* (New York: Farrar, Straus and Giroux, 1968), 139–40.

6 Susie Steiner, "Top Five Regrets of the Dying," *The Guardian*, February 1, 2012, https://www.theguardian.com/lifeandstyle/2012/feb/01/top-five-regrets -of-the-dying.

7 David Bentley Hart, *The Experience of God: Being, Consciousness, Bliss* (New Haven, CT: Yale University Press, 2013), 191–92.

8 Cyndi Dale, *Energetic Boundaries: How to Stay Protected and Connected in Work, Love, and Life* (Boulder, CO: Sounds True, Inc., 2011).

9 Jory MacKay, "This Brilliant Strategy Used by Warren Buffett Will Help You Prioritize Your Time," *Inc.*, November 15, 2017, https://www.inc.com/jory -mackay/warren-buffetts-personal-pilot-reveals-billionaires-brilliant-method -for-prioritizing.html.

10 Michael Lewis, "Obama's Way," *Vanity Fair*, October 2012, https://www
.vanityfair.com/news/2012/10/michael-lewis-profile-barack-obama.

11 Roy F. Baumeister and John Tierney, *Willpower: Rediscovering the Greatest
Human Strength* (New York: Penguin, 2011).

12 "Americans check their phones 80 times a day: study," *New York Post*, November 8, 2017, https://nypost.com/2017/11/08/americans-check-their-phones-80-
times-a-day-study.

13 Thuy Ong, "UK Government Will Use Church Spires to Improve Internet
Connectivity in Rural Areas," *The Verge*, February 19, 2018, https://www
.theverge.com/2018/2/19/17027446/uk-government-churches-wifi-internet
-connectivity-rural.

14 Adrian F. Ward, Kristen Duke, Ayelet Gneezy, and Maarten W. Bos, "Brain
Drain: The Mere Presence of One's Own Smartphone Reduces Available
Cognitive Capacity," *Journal of the Association for Consumer Research* 2, no. 2
(April 2017): 140–54, http://www.journals.uchicago.edu/doi/abs/10.1086/
691462.

15 "The Total Audience Report: Q1 2016," Nielsen, June 27, 2016, http://www
.nielsen.com/us/en/insights/reports/2016/the-total-audience-report-q1-2016.html.

16 Olga Khazan, "How Smartphones Hurt Sleep," *The Atlantic*, February 24,
2015, https://www.theatlantic.com/health/archive/2015/02/how-smartphones
-are-ruining-our-sleep/385792.

17 Perri Klass, "Why Handwriting Is Still Essential in the Keyboard Age," June
20, 2016, *New York Times*, https://well.blogs.nytimes.com/2016/06/20/why
-handwriting-is-still-essential-in-the-keyboard-age.

18 Pam A. Mueller and Daniel M. Oppenheimer, "The Pen Is Mightier Than
the Keyboard," *Psychological Science* 25, no. 6 (April 2014): 1159–68,
http://journals.sagepub.com/doi/abs/10.1177/0956797614524581.

19 Robinson Meyer, "To Remember a Lecture Better, Take Notes by Hand," *The
Atlantic*, May 1, 2014, https://www.theatlantic.com/technology/archive/2014
/05/to-remember-a-lecture-better-take-notes-by-hand/361478.

20 Daniel Gilbert, *Stumbling on Happiness* (New York: Vintage, 2007).

21 Robert Bresson, *Notes on the Cinematographer*, translated by Jonathan Griffin
(København: Green Integer Books, 1997).

22 David Foster Wallace, *This Is Water: Some Thoughts, Delivered on a Significant
Occasion, About Living a Compassionate Life* (New York: Little, Brown, and
Company, 2009).

23 Ibid.

24 Leo Babauta, "How I'm Overcoming My Obsession with Constant Self-Improvement," *Fast Company*, March 19, 2015, https://www.fastcompany.com /3043543/how-im-overcoming-my-obsession-with-constant-self-improvement.

25 Caroline Beaton, "Never Good Enough: Why Millennials Are Obsessed with Self-Improvement," *Forbes*, February 25, 2016, https://www.forbes.com/sites /carolinebeaton/2016/02/25/never-good-enough-why-millennials-are-obsessed -with-self-improvement/#cf00d917efa9.

26 Theresa Nguyen et al., "The State of Mental Health in America 2018," *Mental Health America*, 2017, http://www.mentalhealthamerica.net/issues/state -mental-health-america.

27 "Facts & Statistics," *Anxiety and Depression Association of America*, 2016, https://adaa.org/about-adaa/press-room/facts-statistics#.

28 "Impact bias," *Wikipedia*, May 2016, https://en.wikipedia.org/wiki/Impact_bias.

29 Tim Minchin, "Occasional Address," commencement address at University of Western Australia, TimMinchin.com, September 25, 2013, http://www .timminchin.com/2013/09/25/occasional-address.

30 Olivia Solon, "Ex-Facebook President Sean Parker: Site Made to Exploit Human 'Vulnerability,'" *The Guardian*, November 9, 2017, https://www .theguardian.com/technology/2017/nov/09/facebook-sean-parker-vulnerability -brain-psychology.

31 "Eudaimonism," Philosophy Basics, accessed April 6, 2018, https://www .philosophybasics.com/branch_eudaimonism.html.

32 "Okinawa's Centenarians," Okinawa Centenarian Study, accessed April 6, 2018, http://okicent.org/cent.html.

33 Héctor García and Francesc Miralles, *Ikigai: The Japanese Secret to a Long and Happy Life* (New York: Penguin, 2017).

34 Viktor E. Frankl, *Man's Search for Meaning: An Introduction to Logotherapy* (New York: Simon & Schuster, 1984).

35 Jordan B. Peterson, "2017 Personality 12: Phenomenology: Heidegger, Binswanger, Boss," February 20, 2017, video, 46:32, https://www.youtube .com/watch?v=11oBFCNeTAs.

36 Angela Lee Duckworth, "Grit: The Power of Passion and Perseverance," *TED Talks Education*, April 2013, https://www.ted.com/talks/angela_lee_duckworth _grit_the_power_of_passion_and_perseverance#t-184861.

37 Maria Konnikova, "Multitask Masters," *New Yorker*, May 7, 2014, https:// www.newyorker.com/science/maria-konnikova/multitask-masters.

38 Tanya Basu, "Something Called 'Attention Residue' Is Ruining Your Concentration," *The Cut*, January 21, 2016, https://www.thecut.com/2016/01/attention-residue-is-ruining-your-concentration.html.

39 Kent Beck et al., "Manifesto for Agile Software Development," Agile Alliance, http://agilemanifesto.org, accessed July 2, 2018.

40 Carl Sagan, *The Demon-Haunted World: Science as a Candle in the Dark* (New York: Ballantine Books, 1996).

41 Madison Malone-Kircher, "James Dyson on 5,126 Vacuums That Didn't Work—and the One That Finally Did," *New York*, November 22, 2016, http:///nymag.com/vindicated/2016/11/james-dyson-on-5-126-vacuums-that-didnt-work-and-1-that-did.html.

42 W. Edwards Deming, *The New Economics for Industry, Government, and Education* (Boston, MA: MIT Press, 1993).

43 "Albert Einstein," *Wikiquote*, accessed April 6, 2018, https://en.wikiquote.org/wiki/Albert_Einstein#Disputed.

44 Mihaly Csikszentmihalyi, "Flow, the Secret to Happiness," *TED*, February 2004, https://www.ted.com/talks/mihaly_csikszentmihalyi_on_flow.

45 Marcus Aurelius, *Meditations*, trans. Martin Hammond (New York: Penguin, 2006).

46 Jack Zenger and Joseph Folkman, "The Ideal Praise-to-Criticism Ratio," *Harvard Business Review*, March 15, 2013, https://hbr.org/2013/03/the-ideal-praise-to-criticism.

47 Amy Morin, "7 Scientifically Proven Benefits of Gratitude That Will Motivate You to Give Thanks Year-Round," *Forbes*, November 23, 2014, https://www.forbes.com/sites/amymorin/2014/11/23/7-scientifically-proven-benefits-of-gratitude-that-will-motivate-you-to-give-thanks-year-round/#1367405183c0.

48 David Steindl-Rast, "Want To Be Happy? Be Grateful," TED, June 2013, https://www.ted.com/talks/david_steindl_rast_want_to_be_happy_be_grateful.

49 Commonly attributed to Mark Twain.

50 Heinrich Harrer, *Seven Years in Tibet* (New York: TarcherPerigee, 2009).

51 Winnie Yu, "Workplace Rudeness Has a Ripple Effect," *Scientific American*, January 1, 2012, https://www.scientificamerican.com/article/ripples-of-rudeness.

52 Seth Godin, "The First Law of Organizational Thermodynamics," *Seth's Blog*, February 12, 2018, http://sethgodin.typepad.com/seths_blog/2018/02/the-first-law-of-organization-thermodynamics.html.

53 Joshua Fields Millburn, "Goodbye Fake Friends," *The Minimalists*, https://www.theminimalists.com/fake.

54 Sam Cawthorn (@samcawthorn), "The happiest people dont necessarily have the best of everything but they make the most of everything!!!" June 24, 2011, 4:39 PM, tweet.

55 Drake Baer, "Malcolm Gladwell Explains What Everyone Gets Wrong About His Famous '10,000 Hour Rule'," *Business Insider*, June 2, 2014, http://www .businessinsider.com/malcolm-gladwell-explains-the-10000-hour-rule-2014-6.

56 "14 Ways to Be a Happier Person," *Time*, September 18, 2014, http://time .com/collection/guide-to-happiness/4856925/be-happy-more-joy.

57 Jonathan G. Koomey, *Turning Numbers into Knowledge: Mastering the Art of Problem Solving* (Oakland, CA: Analytics Press, 2008).

CONTENT

CONTENT

CONTENT